# HOW TO SURVIVE AND PROSPER THROUGH A MIDLIFE CRISIS

*A Guidebook for Men*

**Weldon Langfield**

**Weldon Langfield Publications**
**Bakersfield, California**

Weldon Langfield Publications
4450 California Ave., Suite 137
Bakersfield, CA 93309

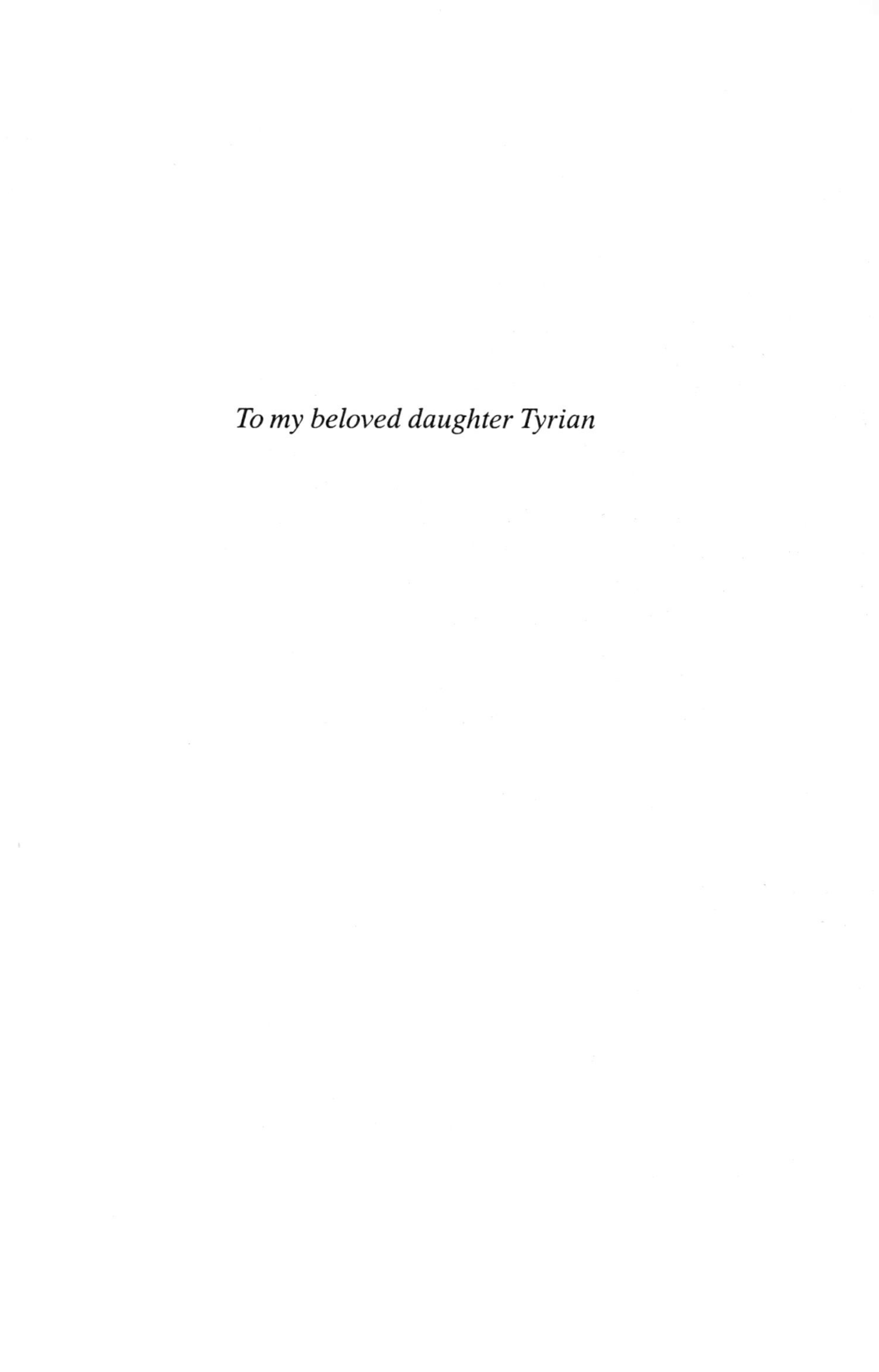

*To my beloved daughter Tyrian*

*If wrinkles must be written upon our brows, let them not be written upon the heart. The spirit should not grow old.*
*—James A. Garfield*

# Contents

# A FRUSTRATING EXPERIMENT

Coming to grips with my fortieth birthday was very difficult. In the year or two preceding it I had feelings of dread, knowing the inevitable was just around the corner. An only child, I was used to getting my own way. However, nothing could slow down the unavoidable aging process.

My wife and I had talked for years of moving to the deep South. We loved the green hills and more family-oriented way of life. We were convinced that the career change accompanying such a move would bear positive fruit. I was a businessman in California and the children were having no problems. In fact, they were quite happy in the Golden State. Yet I dealt with my entry into midlife by hastily pulling up stakes and relocating thousands of miles away.

Six months later we were back in California, chastened but wiser. I had suffered the worst defeat of my life. Other poor decisions were made at that time. While I am ordinarily cautious and slow to make changes, the feeling that something had to be done immediately gripped me at the onset of midlife. Acting on that compelling drive proved very wasteful.

At the onset of my midlife transition several bookstores were searched for a straightforward self-help guide for men facing the birthday which separates the first half of life from the second. If I could have only done some reading, several mistakes might have been avoided. No such book was found, so this brief volume was written to help others in the same situation.

The objective of this book, as the title implies, is not to simply assist the middlescent man in surviving the emotional upheaval that accompanies the beginning of midlife; it is to help him emerge more prosperous and generally better off than if he had not had a midlife crisis.

It is sincerely hoped that this volume benefits all who read it.

## Chapter 1

# WHAT IS A MIDLIFE CRISIS?

*My days are swifter than a weaver's shuttle.*
*—Job 7:6*

Marcus Aurelius said that life is a battle. Instead of a smooth, even journey to a state called "happiness," most of us experience an unpredictable series of peaks and valleys. Graduating from high school and college represent high points in life. Marriage is a high point. The birth of children is a peak experience. Yet between these events are times of disappointment, difficulty, and despair. Job observed, "Man . . . is of few days and full of trouble" (Job 14:1).

The college graduate who realizes for the first time that his philosophy degree will not produce the income he expected feels disappointed. One feels let down when he sees the limits of a paycheck that seemed generous when interviewing for the job. Friction between spouses can be a source of disenchantment. Among potential areas of disappointment is what some researchers call "midlife crisis."

Midlife crisis, which assaults some men around their fortieth birthday, has also been called "male menopause," although many do not consider that term to be accurate. One researcher, for example, pointed out that "male menopause" mistakenly implies a destruction of potency and obscures the real problems of a midlife crisis. The difficulties, then, faced by men during midlife crises are not due to physical changes, as with women in menopause. Many men, however, experience emotional pain.

## Stages of Life

For centuries many have recognized that life can be broken down into stages. Confucius wrote:

> At 15 I set my heart to learning.
> At 30 I planted my feet firmly on the ground.
> At 40 I no longer suffered from perplexities.
> At 50 I knew what were the biddings of heaven.
> At 60 I heard them with docile ear.
> At 70 I could follow the dictates of my own heart . . .

Freud protege Carl Jung was one of the first psychiatrists to suggest that life divides itself into cycles. He compared a man's life span to the sun crossing the sky, writing of "the morning and spring, of the evening and autumn of life."[1] Jung elaborated:

> The one hundred and eighty degrees of the arc of life are divisible into four parts. The first quarter, lying to the east, is childhood—that state in which we are a problem for others, but not yet conscious of any problems of our own. Conscious problems fill out the second and third quarters; while in the

> last—in extreme old age—we descend again into that condition where, unworried by our state of consciousness, we again become something of a problem for others. Childhood and extreme old age, to be sure, are utterly different, and yet they have one thing in common: submersion in unconscious psychic happenings.[2]

Psychiatrist Erik H. Erikson saw life as having eight stages. At each stage one is challenged to develop a certain ego quality, choosing between:

Trust vs. Basic Mistrust
Autonomy vs. Shame and Doubt
Initiative vs. Shame and Guilt
Industry vs. Inferiority
Identity vs. Role Diffusion
Intimacy vs. Isolation
Generativity vs. Stagnation
Ego Integrity vs. Despair[3]

Erikson believed that to attain maturity individuals, when faced with each of those alternatives, must select the first of the two options. While he taught that most of the aforementioned choices are confronted early in life, "Generativity vs. Stagnation" is a challenge faced by maturing individuals. According to Erikson, "Generativity is primarily that interest in establishing and guiding the next generation."[4] The person properly developing in Erikson's scheme, then, desires to help equip younger people, including one's own children, for the tasks of life.

Yale researcher Daniel Levinson likewise theorized that lives divide themselves into distinct stages. Levinson studied men from four occupational groups: hourly workers, executives, biologists and novelists. They were between thirty-five and forty-five years old at the outset of the research. The results were published in a book titled *The*

*Seasons of a Man's Life*. Levinson viewed the life cycle in four stages:

Childhood and adolescence: age 0-22
Early adulthood: age 17-45
Middle adulthood: age 40-65
Late adulthood: age 60-?[5]

Terming the crucial period of change from early adulthood to middle adulthood the "Mid-life Transition," Levinson asserted that it begins at about forty years of age and is initially focused on the past. During the transition a man asks himself probing questions about the value of his life up to that point and concludes that much has been based on illusion. He then undergoes a process Levinson called "de-illusionment," which, as the term suggests, brings him in touch with reality.[6]

As the transition continues, the midlife male begins to emphasize the future and de-emphasize the past. He makes some choices that change his life's structure. Some changes are external in nature, such as a divorce or career move. At the same time he lays the groundwork for his future lifestyle. Internal values are also adjusted during this time. Levinson concluded that a midlife transition has its onset at age forty or forty-one and lasts about five years. In his view, a true midlife transition cannot begin before thirty-eight or after forty-three.

During the midlife transition, according to Levinson, early adulthood must be terminated and the first steps toward initiating middle adulthood must be made. That involves eliminating the negative features of life thus far and testing new choices.[7] As he deals with these and faces areas of internal conflict, a man grows in what Levinson calls "individuation."

Levinson concluded that a midlife transition, which he saw as involving some degree of upheaval, is all but inevitable. He wrote, "Often, a man who has accomplished his goals comes to feel trapped; his success is meaningless and he is now caught within a stultifying situation. Many men find their lives relatively satisfactory in some respects and disappointing or destructive in others."[8] According to Levinson, the emptying nest, the subsequent tension between the husband and wife, and the financial burdens of this period place unavoidable pressure upon a man. This pressure causes a complete reappraisal of his life.[9]

Another well-known advocate of the "stages of life" viewpoint is Gail Sheehy, whose best-seller *Passages* is based on Levinson's research. Sheehy collected 115 "life stories" from America's "pacesetter group," which she defined as "healthy, motivated people who either began in or have entered the middle class, though some began in poverty."[10] Sheehy concluded from her studies that a midlife crisis is inevitable. If one allows himself this crisis, after forty-five he will be ready to "accept entry to middle-age and enjoy its many prerogatives."[11] She wrote that those who "wing it past this midstation . . . [by] denying the downside, . . . [who] play more tennis and run more laps, give bigger parties, seek better hair transplants and higher face lifts" lose the chance for personal development.[12]

In fact, Sheehy concluded that failing to face a midlife crisis can cause the development of an inflexible personality during the fifth decade of life. One arriving at his fiftieth birthday, "having ignored the opportunity for reassessment in midlife passages may take the familiar mulish stance of a protector of the status quo. It is no mistake that such people are called 'diehards.' "[13] Her concept is similar to that of researcher Barbara Fried who wrote, "The crisis is a normal aspect of growth, as natural . . . as teething is for a younger age group."[14]

Those who advocate the "stages of life" view see midlife as almost always tumultuous. Sheehy wrote, "Depression, sexual promiscuity, power chasing, hypochondria, self-destructive acts (alcoholism, drug taking, car accidents, suicide), and violent swings of mood . . . are well documented as rising during the middle years."[15] A catalyst for such dismal behavior is that half of one's life is gone. Less time remains to live than has been lived.

And so it goes. Adultery, divorces, and sudden decisions to walk off jobs held for decades are unavoidable, or nearly so, according to that school of thought. The forty-two-year-old man who abruptly leaves his wife and three kids, starts wearing gold chains, buys a red sports car, and dates women young enough to be his daughter is not fully responsible for what he is doing, according to such theorists.

## Is a Midlife Crisis Really Inevitable?

Not all researchers are convinced that the beginning of midlife *must* be accompanied by a crisis. Psychologist Norma Haan wrote, "Helping professionals may do clients a disservice by expecting them to be either crisis-ridden or unable to adopt new ways of living and coping."[16] Questioning the validity of the interviews behind Levinson's and Sheehy's conclusions, Haan stated:

> These accounts draw their themes from life stories told retrospectively by people who were willing to cooperate with the opportunity to relate their experiences to an interested and expert listener. This approach has a certain value because of the

> free flow of expression can bring aspects of self and living to the fore. But it is also limited by everyone's proclivity to experience his or her own life as a drama.[17]

Researchers Michael Farrell and Stanley Rosenberg concluded that Levinson's findings were based on a self-selected group—individuals who felt enough stress to seek help for their emotional problems. The researchers pointed out that if only 5-10% percent of the population sought therapy for midlife distress, it would appear to the professional counselor as "a virtual tidal wave of distress or pathology." They further suggested that since most of Levinson's subjects were from the intellectual and creative elite, results may only apply to highly creative and intelligent men.[18]

Farrell and Rosenberg pointed out that Erikson's hypothesis of stages of life, if true, would imply *greater* strength at middle-age to cope with any midlife crisis. They wrote, "Having had more time to confront issues of the later life cycle, middle-aged men should be at least potentially more 'mature' and show more signs of integration than younger men."[19]

They concluded that their own findings do not support well-defined stages of life but rather "halting, sporadic, more and less workable attempts by men to create a self they can value."[20] Similarly, clinical psychologist Diane Medved totally rejected the concept of a midlife crisis, writing, "The term 'mid-life crisis' is not only over-rated, its exulted, and all this does is excuse a great deal of despicable behavior."[21]

In light of these comments and findings the obvious question is, "Is there a midlife crisis at all?" Farrell and Rosenberg determined that only 12% of respondents they polled manifested what could fairly be called a "crisis." They did, however, conclude that 50% "either externalize . . . frustration and despair or seek to hide it."[22]

Clearly, while the midlife transition does not always reach crisis proportions, over half of all men beginning midlife have feelings of frustration and despair. According to Farrell and Rosenberg, a majority of middle-aged men do not find entry into midlife smooth sailing. Other evidence supports that conclusion.

For example, psychosomatic illness shows a sharp increase at midlife. Peptic ulcers have their highest incidence in the 40-50 age group. Hypertension and heart disease are also much more common for those in middle-age than in young adulthood. Statistics show an increase in depression, which can help produce ulcers, retard healing, and even cause premature aging in men about forty years of age. Those problems may well reflect the anxiety experienced by the midlife male who is too occupied with evaluating his past and future to enjoy a tranquil present.

## Negative Emotions at Midlife

While the term "crisis" can only describe 12% of the male population, most men experience significant negative emotions at midlife. What is it that triggers feelings ranging from alienation in 12% to despair or frustration in 50%? The aging process evokes such emotions. Midlife is a glaring reminder of one's mortality.

Physically, the evidence of decline is abundant. Hair starts to gray and thin while muscle tone begins to noticeably decline. Body fat is redistributed downward. Weight is easy to gain and difficult to lose. Loss of physical strength and stamina is noticeable, though modest. Bifocals often

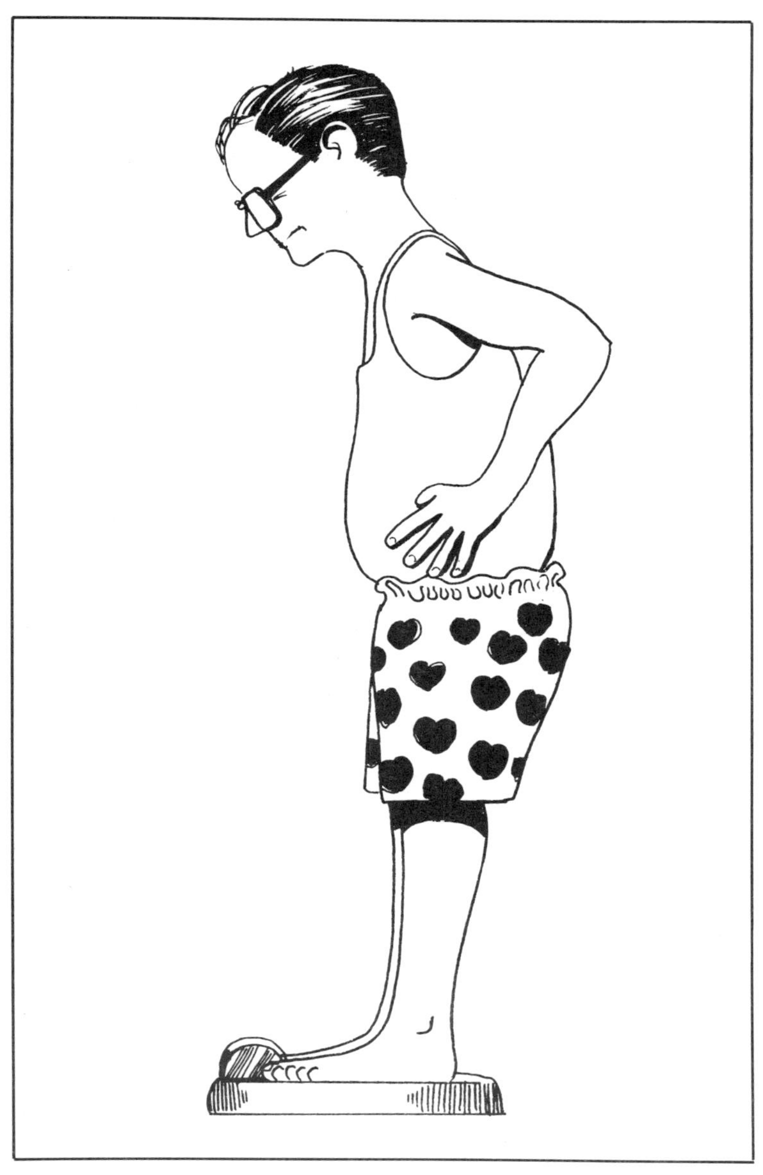

*Physically, the evidence of decline is abundant.*

publicly testify to deteriorating eyesight. Wrinkles are more noticeable and skin that has been overexposed to the sun begins to show inordinate aging, looseness, and color changes.

The frequency of illness increases. Kidney functioning in the forty-year-old man is at 85% of its peak. Lung capacity is similarly lessened. Hearing has been diminishing since about age twenty-eight, though mostly in ranges other than that of the human voice. Skin becomes thinner and flatter. The overall regression in the human body, by one estimate, is around 1% each year after thirty.[23] In short, by age forty, every glance in the mirror and every episode of physical exertion provides tangible evidence of one's mortality.

Interestingly enough, blue-collar workers believe the onset of middle-age begins as early as thirty, while white-collar workers believe it begins closer to fifty. That is probably because the laborer is more dependent on physical strength and keenly notices the loss of vitality. Even for the man who works with his hands, the decline in vigor is modest and does not substantially affect productivity or lifestyle. This slight weakening is often perceived, however, as cataclysmic. It is seen not only as a loss of masculine strength but, more importantly, as a harbinger of feebleness and death.

The process of crossing the threshold to middle-age is made more difficult by our culture's obsession with youth. Some societies revere and honor their aged, giving them a special place as the guardians of tradition. But Jung observed, "For the most part, our old people try to compete with the young. In the United States it is almost an ideal for the father to be the brother of his sons, and for the mother if possible to be the youngest sister of her daughter."[24]

Self esteem for many Americans is tied to youthfulness. "Good looking" is equated with "young looking." Those who model clothing, play glamorous roles in movies, and sell toothpaste and deodorant on television are young and energetic. Consequently, many go to great lengths to maintain a youthful appearance, getting "new hairstyles, new hair, new wardrobes, and new partners."[25]

Surprisingly, there is a bright side to the physical decline. The frequency of accidents goes down at forty. Additionally, the number of disabled people in the forty-to-sixty range is only a little higher than in young adulthood.[26]

## Positive Aspects of Midlife

While the capacity to learn massive amounts of information has diminished by the fortieth year, other intellectual functions grow so as to more than offset the decrease. The vocabulary of a forty-five year old man is three times what it was when he was twenty. The brain of a sixty-year-old possesses almost four times as much knowledge as it did when he was twenty-one.[27]

Psychologically, the midlife male is better equipped to handle many types of problems. He has more emotional and mental equipment to effectively deal with the world than at any previous age. However, the second half of life may bring about a decline in job interest, because at that age a career no longer provides a primary source of satisfaction it once did.

Some researchers see midlife as a time when what some call "feminine traits" emerge. Jung compared the attributes of masculinity and femininity to a store of substances. A man uses a large portion of his masculine substance during his first years and begins in later years to draw more heavily on his feminine substance. He may become more passive at home while his wife may adopt a more assertive role. (In my view, what is taken as the emergence of female traits is simply the broadening and mellowing of the personality and has nothing to do with masculinity or femininity.)

The emergence of the so-called feminine side of one's personality may result in previously-suppressed artistic urges. The creative capacity may make itself known for the first time, motivating the midlife male to pursue more aesthetic endeavors. On the other hand, that capacity may again be suppressed, never to be heard from again.

The midlife male has the physical and intellectual means to more than survive the early forties. It is no wonder that power in our society rests in the hands of those in midlife.

## Disappointment in Achievements at Midlife

At forty years of age, most men have less time to live than they have already lived. Even substantial achievements sometimes seem insignificant in light of the opportunities and potential that the first half of life offered. One author observed:

> Something paradoxical occurs when the executive gets his promotion, the banker his raise, the salesman his franchise, and the teacher his tenure. The battle won, each man expects to feel victorious. Instead, there is a sense of loss. Is this all there is? he wonders.[28]

Many youthful dreams are finally seen to be unattainable and deep remorse often accompanies their passing.

Longfellow expressed the despair shared by multitudes at midlife when he wrote in *Mezzo Cammin:*

> Half of my life is gone, and I have let
> The years slip from me and have not fulfilled
> The aspirations of my youth, to build
> Some tower of song with lofty parapet . . .
> Though, half-way up the hill, I see the Past
> Lying beneath me with its sounds and sights,
> A city in the twilight dim and vast,
> With smoking roofs, soft hills, and gleaming lights,
> And hear above me on the autumnal blast
> The cataract of Death far thundering from the heights.

Surprisingly, feelings of disappointment and questions of the significance of achievements haunt even those who have realized virtually all their dreams. Yet the middle-aged man has paid the price of half of a lifetime for his achievements. What accomplishment, no matter how grand, is worth 50% of a unique, irreplaceable life span? One successful attorney put it this way: "I've been braced for life becoming momentous, but mostly it has only gotten complicated."[29] King Solomon, who possessed unimaginable wealth, recognized the futility of acquisition and achievement, writing in Ecclesiastes, "Vanity of vanities, says the Preacher, vanity of vanities; all is vanity" (Ecclesiastes 1:2).

Most of us are not superstars in our professions. Some of our aspirations remain unfulfilled at midlife. We must face sobering realities, realities which force us to take stock. While probably not at our peak in earning power, at forty we can usually see where our peak will be. A man climbing the corporate latter who finds himself sidetracked in a middle management position knows he will probably never be a top executive. The educator in an obscure university will likely never have a tenured position at a leading institution. The minister who is not serving a high-profile congregation in a large city will most likely never have that opportunity.

Researcher Beric Wright observed that often individuals "react with acute depressions when they realize that they have achieved a great deal but failed at the last fence. They have not, as Disraeli said of politics, got to the top of the greasy pole."[30] In 1640, George Herbert wrote in *Jacula Prudentum,* "He that is not handsome at twenty, nor strong at thirty, nor rich at forty, nor wise at fifty, will never be handsome, strong, rich, or wise." Midlife is a time to take stock, and the disparity that emerges between career achievements and expectations can be a source of bitter disappointment. Levinson wrote:

> If a man at 40 has failed to realize his most cherished dreams, he must begin to come to terms with the failure and arrive at a new set of choices around which to rebuild his life. If he has succeeded brilliantly, he must consider the meaning and value of his success.[31]

Successful or not, the midlife male has much to think about, and such contemplation often leads to feelings of melancholy, anxiety, and despair. Interestingly, the disappointment experienced by the man who gets what he wants is not too different from the disappointment felt by the man who does not.

## Sources of Stress at Midlife

As we have seen, many mid-life males ponder lost opportunities and are disappointed with their careers. Many are distraught as they dwell on the seemingly imminent specter of death. Financial concerns in particular usually reach a peak for those who have experienced two decades of adulthood. The midlife male must support his wife and one or two teenage children, who may soon require expensive higher education. He is usually at least a partial care-giver to his aging parents. With a growing income, his share of taxes sometimes makes him think he is supporting half of western civilization.

Finally, at midlife, many men suffer tension as they come to terms with the aforementioned "feminine" side of their personalities. The executive may suddenly want to become a novelist; the factory worker finds himself deeply interested in oil painting; the entrepreneur longs to compose music. Talents may have been suppressed or ignored so that a career could be built, but the midlife male finds himself ready to explore and develop them.

Other circumstances can make the transition into midlife even more burdensome than it might otherwise be. Entry into the middle years is particularly devastating for the man who has lost his job. Likewise, the employee with a dead-end job may experience greater frustration than he otherwise would.

Family problems, a significant source of anxiety, are often at their zenith at midlife. Children are usually teenagers by now and present new challenges and discipline problems. Outright rebellion of one or more children may rule out the possibility of an idyllic family life. Raising a family is the most costly at midlife.

The relationship between spouses is usually at its lowest ebb at midlife. The quality of marriage begins to decline when children enter the home and continues until they start leaving, at which point it improves.[32] This means that for the man at midlife, marriage may be at its bleakest.

Such conditions can produce bouts of depression and anxiety. Additionally, they lead to periods of deep self-examination. Too often, the conclusion after intense introspection is that life has been an utter disappointment.

An overwhelming sense of failure and powerlessness, however, is not necessarily an accurate gauge of how things really are. The cliché "no pain, no gain" reminds us that even changes for the better involve some stress. One author put it this way: "The man who feels as if his life is in shambles can take comfort from the fact that his painful flounderings are probably signs of growth: his world is shaking because he's gotten too big for it."[33]

## Midlife Despair—An Indication of Growth

The above subheading is a major premise of this book. Feelings of disappointment, failure, and alienation at the beginning of midlife do not necessarily reflect reality. Just because a man *feels* like a loser does not necessarily mean he *is* one. Rather, he may feel that way because he has genuinely outgrown his job and goals. Such emotions may simply signal that it is time to fashion a new life. The manner in which the midlife male reacts to those feelings, and not the feelings themselves, will have much to do with the shape of his future.

If he responds to them by escaping into a lifestyle that offers short-term comfort and long-term grief, negative emotions are for him the beginning of far bleaker times. For example, the man who leaves an otherwise happy home to chase blondes twenty years his junior is sowing seeds of heartache which must be reaped in a few years.

The person who reacts to despair over his lack of achievement by making hasty investment decisions aimed at suddenly catapulting him to wealth is probably in for an education. He will soon learn what financial failure really is. The man who deals with midlife melancholy by blaming it on the first thing or person that comes to mind selects escapism over growth. He will by that behavior prepare himself for years of discontent.

Reacting to midlife blues by remaining in what has become an unrewarding and boring rut will likely lead to far greater dissatisfaction in a few years. Such a man will live out his old age saying, "If I had only taken that chance," or asking himself, "What if I had taken the risk when I had the opportunity?"

On the other hand, one who interprets despair and frustration as growing pains and acts accordingly can not only endure but prosper through a midlife transition. He must be like the contrarian of the investment world—staunchly refusing to let emotions rule his actions, he must instead make intellect his master. Using his mind, he can objectively and creatively identify ways to craft a new life with the capacity to accommodate his growth.

While many of his friends are walking off jobs, or getting divorced, or gambling the family jewels on half-baked business ventures, the wise midlife male will stand back and take an objective look at his alternatives. Then, at the proper time, he will act deliberately and cautiously. By behaving in this manner, he will emerge from the midlife crisis happier and more prosperous than when he entered it.

---

[1]C.G. Jung, *Modern Man in Search of a Soul* (San Diego, California: Harcourt Brace Jovanovich, 1933), 107.

[2]Ibid., 113.

[3]Erik H. Erikson, *Childhood and Society* (New York: W. W. Norton & Co., 1950), 219-234.

[4]Ibid., 9-14, 231.

[5]Daniel J. Levinson, *The Seasons of a Man's Life* (New York: Ballantine Books, 1978), 9-14, 18.

[6]Ibid., 192-193.

[7]Ibid.,191-192.

[8]Ibid., 31.

[9]Ibid., 23-32.

[10]Gail Sheehy, *Passages. Predictable Crises of Adult Life* (New York: Bantam Books, 1976), 23-24.

[11]Ibid., 375.

[12]Ibid., 363.

[13]Ibid., 496.

[14]Barbara Fried, *The Middle-Age Crisis* (New York: Harper and Row, 1967), 7.

[15]Sheehy, Passages, 358.

[16]Norma Haan, "Personality at Midlife," in *Midlife Myths. Issues, Findings, and Practice Implications* ed. Ski Hunter and Martin Sundel (Newbury Park, California: Sage Publications, 1989), 155.

[17]Ibid., 148.

[18]Michael P. Farrell and Stanley D. Rosenberg, *Men at Midlife* (Boston: Auburn House Publishing Co., 1981), 12-13, 23.

[19]Ibid., 56.

[20]Ibid., 12-13.

[21]Diane Medved, *The Case Against Divorce* (New York: Ivy Books, 1989), 89.

[22]Farrell and Rosenberg, *Men at Midlife*, 88.

[23]William H. Van Hoose, *Midlife Myths and Realities* (Atlanta: Humanics Limited, 1985), 16-19.

[24]Jung, *Modern Man*, 110.

[25]Van Hoose, *Midlife Myths*, 3.

[26]Ibid., 19-20.

[27]Ibid., 37.

[28]Nancy Mayer, *The Male Mid-life Crisis: Fresh Start After Forty* (New York: Doubleday & Co., 1978), 61.

[29]Lawrence Shames, "Has the Thirty- and Fortysomething Generation Passed Its Peak?" *Utne Reader*, January-February 1990, 78.

[30]H. Peter Hildebrand, "Psychological Problems of the Over Forties," in *After Forty—The Time for Achievement?* ed. Gary L. Cooper and Derek P. Torrington (Chichester, England: John Wiley and Sons, 1981), 19.

[31]Levinson, *Seasons*, 30.

[32]Boyd C. Rollins, "Marital Quality at Midlife," in *Midlife Myths. Issues, Findings*, 187.

[33]Mayer, *Mid-life Crisis*, 35-36.

## Chapter 2

# "DON'TS" OF A MIDLIFE CRISIS

*A prudent man foresees evil and hides himself,*
*But the simple pass on and are punished.*
*—Proverbs 22:3*

New pressures bear down on the man undergoing a midlife transition. These anxieties can lead to devastating consequences. Some men walk off jobs held for decades and leave wives that have been faithful partners for many years. Some men alienate their children by very childish behavior. Others make a poor series of choices at midlife that irreversibly mangles their careers, destroys their family lives, and leaves them financially crippled.

Many of us feel the weight of forty years upon our bodies and spirits. Perhaps we cannot avoid sinking into the abyss of regret as the seemingly feeble rewards of two decades of hard work are considered. What we can avoid is making a chain of woeful decisions as we react to the unchangeable reality that the past may not have been as kind to us as we would have liked. We can resist choices destined to leave us and our loved ones lonely, impoverished, and emotionally scarred. Maybe we cannot help being saddened by the seeming fruitlessness of our labors. We can, however, avoid choosing a new direction certain to lead us into emotional and material poverty.

This volume is intended to do more than assist in avoiding foolish decisions; it is written to point the reader toward a better life. The Bible character Job emerged wiser and richer for all his trials. Our goal is to likewise emerge more stable, mature, and prosperous after the storm clouds of the fourth decade of life give way to azure skies. In pursuit of that goal, this chapter will deal with some "don'ts," that is, some things to avoid during a midlife crisis.

## Don't Make Sudden Changes

The Bible says, "He sins who hastens with his feet" (Proverbs 19:2). It is wise to refrain from impulsive, ill-considered decisions, especially during times of emotional upheaval. At age forty I thought my problems would be solved by living somewhere else. Tennessee was the place to which my wife and I decided to relocate. I knew trips back to California for business purposes would be necessary. Although I had not done much business travel, it seemed certain that I would be able to tolerate such a schedule. I was wrong and underestimated the resulting strain on my family. Instead of adapting to the new schedule, I spent nearly two seeks a month trying to transact business on the West Coast while feeling very depressed.

Additionally, the effect a move would have on my two teenaged children was underestimated. Raised in the casual environment of California, they suddenly had to deal with the more formal ways of a major southern city. The schools were on a different academic track and the classroom was imbued with a decorum to which they were not accustomed.

People dressed more formally; some actually wore suits to football games. In California a man does well to wear a suit to a funeral! We all experienced culture shock which, naively, was unexpected. During my two weeks a month in Tennessee I tried to establish a business. Unfortunately, I had even underestimated the competition in that area.

All things considered, the decision to move was ill-conceived. Many such moves in midlife yield similar results. One writer called midlife crisis "the frantic forties." She wrote of men in the throes of a transition, "Certain that at any moment they will be over the hill, they are likely to dash out with a 'last chance' and do something foolish."[1]

When approaching my fortieth birthday I felt very much in a rut, and very disappointed with the meager accomplishments years of hard work had yielded. It seemed certain that a relocation would solve my problems. Yet I found that "no matter how spectacular the setting, the man who transplants himself with the hope of shedding a loathsome self will ultimately discover that there is no utopia so magical it will release him from his own skin."[2]

We considered our plans for quite a while. A little more time invested carefully checking out the situation at our planned destination would have been well spent. To move two thousand miles only to come back six months later cost time, emotional energy, and money. Since returning, I have encountered others who pulled up stakes to go to "idyllic" locations only to settle again on home turf in less than a year.

Before moving to the place of your dreams, whether it be a sparsely furnished white frame house in a Maine fishing village, or a log home in the green hills of East Tennessee, or a sunlit condominium in Florida, thoroughly investigate. You may say, "Once we get in that farmhouse in Pennsylvania, we will be happy." That is what everybody says. Save yourself a lot of trouble and investigate beforehand. Spend a couple of vacations there. Research the economy and make sure there will be no financial surprises you cannot handle. Remember, the standard of living varies significantly from one region to the other.

Expect cultural differences and try to identify and prepare for them before relocating. Experience the seasons and climate of the area before committing yourself. I know several Californians, spoiled by dry and temperate weather, who have moved east only to return because of the snow in the winter and the humidity in the summer. Make sure you spend some time in the area during its most severe seasons.

If you have children, realistically evaluate the impact a move will have on them. During teenage years, even the most gregarious kids have trouble making new friends. Think about how your ability to care for aged parents will be affected.

If you relocate, rent a house for several months after arriving in the new area. After becoming more familiar with the locale, you can better decide where to live permanently. If things do not work out and you decide to return home, you will not be stuck with a real estate "investment" that has to be handled long distance, usually a quick way to experience several thousand dollars worth of negative prosperity.

Don't burn your bridges. When you have weighed everything you can think of, realize that there still may be a fly in the ointment you will discover later. Just as every place has advantages, each has certain drawbacks. There will likely be some adverse surprises in spite of your best efforts at planning and preparation.

When in the throes of a midlife crisis, there is a tendency to make swift, emotion-charged choices. Don't add to your anxieties the many problems that come with shuttling across the country in vain.

## Don't Commit Adultery

Marital unfaithfulness is reaching epidemic proportions in the United States. Various surveys indicate that between 30-70% of men and 25-50% of women succumb to its siren call. Yet it is not a matter of "everyone is doing it." One researcher concluded that "optimal functioning men with good mental health tend to have good marriages at middle age."[3] Unfortunately, many midlife men do not have the inner strength to resist adultery. Certain things can cause a person to think that his existence will be improved by having an affair.

### Reasons for Adultery

***Various changes in the dynamics of his marriage are sometimes used by the midlife male as a pretense for cheating.*** After twenty years of marriage, the wife is usually behaving more autonomously than ever before. Some men have a hard time dealing with a spouse who is increasingly independent. Additionally, during the child-rearing years, the wife may have become engrossed in raising the children while her husband was deeply involved in advancing his career. The two of them discover at midlife that they have grown apart.

***Some men become unfaithful because of "scapegoatism."*** When life is not what it should be it is much easier to blame someone else. The boss, secretary, or parents may be blamed. A man may blame younger, more energetic colleagues for his failure to realize his potential. He may fault office politics, welfare recipients, or minorities. Usually, however, he blames his wife. He says to himself, "If only she had been more supportive," or "If only she had a college education," or "If only she had more social grace." Thus the entire burden of a failed career or unsatisfying life is shifted to her.

It seems incredible that the foibles of a spouse are enough to completely neutralize an otherwise perfect life, but that is the way some people reason. One observer wrote, "Otherwise sensible men suddenly grant their mates extraordinary demonic powers during this period."[4]

***Some men seize upon adultery in the frenzied search for a fountain of youth.*** They feel sure that the vigor of the past can be recaptured through relationships with younger women.

***Monotony in marriage is sometimes used to justify adultery.*** Yet it is only a symptom of more serious problems. Boredom is frequently a veneer covering deeper concerns about middle age, such as fears of aging and death. One author wrote of midlife marital ennui, "Trying to get rid of it with a small dose of sexual appeal is like trying to cure an advanced case of anorexia nervosa with a handful of chocolate kisses."[5] Yet there are those who believe novelty will diminish the effects of a midlife transition.

***Some husbands evidently become too successful for their lifelong mates.*** A 1985 study concluded that men who earned more than $60,000 per year had a 70% possibility of committing adultery. Another survey indicated a 70% incidence of adultery for men earning $70,000 or more in 1986.[6] To restate those statistics in terms not dated by inflation, seven out of ten husbands in the top 3% of earnings commit adultery. Some men, as they achieve new career highs, come to feel that their wives are not quite good enough for their new status. A new playmate is selected to go along with the new prosperity.

***The "do what feels good" attitude of the seventies has given rise to much adultery.*** Some psychologists actually claim that an affair can help a marriage. One author, writing in 1978, suggested that when a husband announces that he has fallen in love with another woman, the perceptive wife can improve the union by turning her spouse's new capacity for feeling back into the marriage. The writer related the case history of a couple, Fred and Donna, who each had an affair. Within a few months they chose to reunite and were happier than ever before. The conclusion was this: "If there is a basic bond of warm feelings, it is possible for a couple to come together on a deeper, more honest basis when the crisis ends."[7] Other articles and books from the 1970s reflect the same thinking.

Even if there are instances of couples improving their marriage by cheating (which this writer seriously doubts), they are rare exceptions and not the norm. An affair is almost always a tragedy which at best permanently scars a marriage and at worse causes divorce. One psychologist observed, "Once the line of sexual infidelity is crossed, it will require great effort to maintain accountability and reestablish trust. Many couples decide that the effort is either futile or too difficult, so they opt for divorce."[8]

***The image of adultery in the movies and on TV contributes to unfaithfulness.*** Hollywood has bombarded us with the notion that an affair is a humorous little indiscretion with no significant negative consequences. In fact, I just saw a commercial for a movie about a married lawyer who was having an affair with his best friend's wife and a total stranger at the same time. His wife and the other women were shown laughing and seemingly enjoying life to the fullest.

The idea suggested by that and similar movies and television shows could not be farther from the truth. Adultery harms the innocent spouse by making her life miserable. It harms the straying partner by destroying his character. Adultery cripples a marriage by demolishing its foundation of trust.

***Immaturity causes philandering.*** Some husbands (and wives, for that matter) feel overly taxed by the responsibility of adult relationships. The daily grind of working, mowing the lawn, shopping, keeping the car maintained, etc., becomes for them too much of a burden. The shallow sometimes commit adultery to escape from routine living.

## Why Avoid Adultery?

***Adultery springs from weakness.*** While today's society scorns practically any moral judgments, the fact remains that "fooling around" springs from emotional weakness, not strength. Psychoanalyst Herbert S. Stream wrote,

"Anything but a monogamous marriage is immature and unhealthful."[9] He further declared:

> An extramarital liaison is an expression of unresolved homosexual, incestuous, dependency, and sadomasochistic conflicts . . . Since the motives for affairs go much deeper than the desire for sexual gratification, those who decide to engage in such activities will not find them rewarding. Professional help is really what they need.[10]

***Adultery harms the moral fiber of the participants.*** At the marriage ceremony vows are taken in which both bride and groom promise permanent monogamy. The wandering partner by breaking his word compromises his integrity. A successful marriage is based on trust, and trust presupposes exclusivity. The adulterer grossly violates that trust.

Integrity is further compromised by the lying and manipulation used to hide an affair. To have time to meet his lover, the adulterer may say he has to work late or take a business trip. Lies are used to explain why a motel key is found in a pocket or why a vacation must be canceled. An affair thus reduces an otherwise sincere person to a fraud. He not only hurts himself by renouncing his integrity, he will likely feel guilty and anxious in the course of the affair. The guilt springs from the knowledge that he is doing wrong, the anxiety from fear of being found out.[11]

***Adultery degrades the unfaithful husband as well as his partners.*** The cheating spouse relates to his accomplices by animal instinct instead of respect and love. Sex becomes a source of personal gratification instead of a medium of bonding and communication between two people with a lifetime commitment.

***Adultery makes a fool out of the adulterer.*** The middle-aged man is well beyond dating years; to be carried away with infatuation typical of the high school set looks more than a little ludicrous. In the words of one writer, "Forty is not fourteen." She continued, "Most of us would have to admit that at our age we make rotten star-crossed lovers, anyway . . . we are aware that even passion, the most humorless of emotions, can be ridiculous."[12]

For many adulterers, the only real attraction of an affair is the "forbidden fruit" appeal. Many have noticed that when their lovers suggest marriage, the affair loses its appeal and excitement.

***Adultery will almost always cause more pain for the person who commits it than he would have otherwise felt.*** An undercurrent of tension results from the realization that the fling will eventually be discovered. Some deceive themselves into believing that there is no longer an unwelcome, dreaded tomorrow. The truth is tomorrow will come, and added to its burdens will be the tragedy of marital unfaithfulness. One woman said, "I was desperate to get away from Gene because I was in so much pain, but the affair only increased my misery."[13]

If you want to add to the pain of your midlife transition, an affair is for you. You will introduce into your marriage a whole rainbow of bitter emotions. Anger, hatred, guilt, pain, humiliation, and confusion have all been linked to unfaithfulness.

***Adultery deeply hurts the innocent spouse.*** The brunt of grief from an affair is borne by the innocent partner. She may not even be aware that there was a problem in the marriage. All of a sudden, however, she is confronted with the truth that the relationship has been breached in the most fundamental way possible.

Upon discovering her husband's infidelity, the wife feels very inadequate. Since she is only one of at least two of his bed partners, she feels cheapened by the affair. She is consumed by feelings of loneliness. Before the affair it was she and her husband against the world. There was something exclusive and unique between them. They had a special attachment that set their relationship apart from that which they had with siblings, parents, children, and friends.

Now the faithful wife discovers that the supposed specialness of the liaison was one-sided. She was honoring the union but her husband was not. It never was her and her spouse against the world after all, but her alone. The "all for one and one for all" spirit that she thought the marriage was built upon did not even exist. The wife was allowed to believe there was far more to the marriage than there really was. In a word, her marriage has lost its innocence. She now feels a combination of sadness, hurt, anger, confusion, guilt, depression, and loneliness.[14] One therapist pointed out that when one's mate is hurt, the promiscuous spouse also loses. He wrote:

> This would be akin to the doubles tennis player who wants to avenge the fact that the partner is not playing the preferred style. Rather than discussing how to successfully blend their strategies, the frustrated partner repeatedly trips the other. Perhaps dominance or punishment is conveyed, but the team loses.[15]

***Adultery usually damages and sometimes completely destroys a man's influence with his children.*** When offspring, especially teenagers, realize what is taking place, they usually react with enough resentment to create a permanent rift between themselves and their father. Remember, Erikson said that the maturing adult should be concerned about generativity, that is, helping the upcoming generation prepare to take its place in society. One researcher wrote:

> Perhaps the most useful and important thing the father or mother can do is to provide a worthy pattern for the adolescent to follow—a pattern of the good father or mother, the good husband or wife, the good homemaker, and the good citizen.[16]

Fulfilling that role effectively can best be done only by one who exercises self-control and attempts to grow in his marriage.

***Adultery proves nothing about one's virility.*** Midlife men often question their masculinity at the first signs their bodies are declining. Some chase women in search of tangible evidence that they are still attractive. For some in the baby boom generation, the ability to "score" in high school and college days was, in some circles, considered proof of one's desirability.

Of course, promiscuity was less common several decades ago than it is today. This country has since undergone the "sexual revolution." The "free love" era has come and gone. Incurable, deadly social diseases have reached epidemic levels in the United States. Cohabitation without the benefit of matrimony used to be rare; now it is commonplace. Sex outside of marriage today proves nothing about one's virility.

Clearly, the person who wants to survive and prosper during his midlife transition will avoid adultery at any cost. Solomon wrote, "Whoever commits adultery with a woman lacks understanding; he who does so destroys his own soul" (Proverbs 6:32). The object of the strategy proposed in this book is to emerge a better person, not to come forth with far more personal problems than at the onset of the midlife crisis.

Extra-marital sex can be avoided first of all by realizing that it usually begins with mild flirtations which gradually expand until a full-blown affair is underway. The tendency of many who cheat is to claim that "it just happened," as though it were an unpreventable accident. Such is never the case. One writer observed:

> Early on in an extramarital friendship, there often comes a moment of "maybe." Even when your friendship is altogether innocent, your friend may send the signal, or you may sense the feeling, of further possibility. It occurs in a glance more meaningful than mere friends exchange.[17]

There is a point, then, at which the straying partner could have easily said "enough" and ended the development of the affair. Adultery is never unforeseen and unexpected. Caution must be exercised to identify and prune improper feelings before they blossom.

Care must be taken to interpret communications problems between spouses as a challenge to improve the marriage rather than as a blank check to seek satisfaction beyond its bounds. Resisting adultery testifies to one's maturity, stability and depth of character.

***Last but certainly not least, adultery is displeasing to God.*** The seventh of the Ten Commandments declares, "You shall not commit adultery" (Exodus 20:14). Knowing how destructive marital unfaithfulness is, God further warns:

> Can a man take fire to his bosom,
> And his clothes not be burned?
> Can one walk on hot coals,
> And his feet not be seared?

> So is he who goes in to his neighbor's wife;
> Whoever touches her shall not be innocent
> (Proverbs 6:27-29).

Solomon continued, "Whoever commits adultery with a woman lacks understanding; he who does so destroys his own soul. Wounds and dishonor he will get, and his reproach will not be wiped away" (Proverbs 6:32-33). Paul indicated that those who commit adultery cannot go to heaven when he wrote, "Neither fornicators, nor idolaters, nor adulterers . . . will inherit the kingdom of God" (1 Corinthians 6:9-10).

The Hebrew letter says, "Fornicators and adulterers God will judge" (Hebrews 13:4). Peter indicated that marital unfaithfulness was characteristic, not of faithful Christians, but of godless heretics whom he described as having "eyes full of adultery and that cannot cease from sin" (2 Peter 2:14).

The midlife male must avoid marital unfaithfulness.

## Don't Divorce

There can be good cause for one to part ways with his spouse. He may feel the adultery of his mate has so deeply scarred the marriage there is no hope he can ever live in the relationship without great pain. Christ himself understood that, stating, "Whoever divorces his wife, except for sexual immorality, and marries another, commits adultery" (Matthew 19:9).

I am acquainted with one woman who divorced her spouse when he combined repeated trysts with substance abuse. She was concerned not only with the lack of respect her husband's immorality implied but also with the influence his cocaine and marijuana use had on their adolescent children. Not all divorces, however, are justified.

## Some Causes of Unnecessary Divorces

***The flippant attitude toward marriage dissolution today has influenced many to divorce.*** Those who divorce for superficial reasons disregard God's will. Malachi stated, "For the Lord God of Israel says that He hates divorce (Malachi 2:16). Some leave because they "need more space," while others simply want "a fresh start." Job promotions may cause some to conclude they have "grown apart" (in other words, the wife has not kept up with the mushrooming sophistication of her lifelong companion). Some leave a marriage in shambles so they can "find themselves."

***Some grow weary of the give-and-take which is a part of any relationship.*** That includes marital, business, or family relationships. I know one couple that came very close to parting ways simply because of differing dispositions. She was an extrovert who enjoyed large gatherings and he was an introvert who avoided them. Imagine: splitting up, selling the house, dividing the assets, and sharing the children for a reason like that! What ever happened to "for better or worse"?

There are rough spots in any alliance that need to be sanded and smoothed with time. That includes business partnerships, co-worker relationships, and married couples. Certain facets of all marriages need to be worked at: relationships with in-laws and parents, the handling of money, and the sharing of household chores.

No two married people are exactly equal in talent, ability, and education. If the husband is a high achiever, the gap between the accomplishments of spouses at the time of the marriage ceremony will probably widen as time passes. If the wife has spent twenty years doing housework and driving the kids to piano lessons while her spouse has acquired more authority on the job and even advanced his education, why is it surprising that there may be a difference between their levels of vocational skill and knowledge? To expect anything less is unrealistic. Is that a bona fide reason for dissolving a marriage?

***Modern America's non-judgmental attitude contributes to divorce.*** Society refuses to judge those who are divorced for any reason, and the legal systems of most states have been reshaped by modern legislation to accommodate such shallow mores. The deed is done so quickly—in six months to a year—that there is little time to adequately reflect on it. Among the reasons given for such a parting of the ways is the midlife crisis. A characteristic of men who find themselves in the throes of a midlife transition is their tendency to reject their more sedentary past and take risks.[18] Sometimes those risks involve a new job, a leap into self-employment, or a move across the country. In other cases they involve divorce and an entirely new life.

***The decline in fixed values is a prime cause of divorce.*** Forty or fifty years ago, when religion was a more important feature of American life, divorces were rare. Today's society has rejected much absolutism. One psychologist declared, "When you aren't sure about God or don't believe in Him, then you do what you want. People then become the source of values, and who is to say that one person's sincere belief is any better than another's?"[19]

Half of all nuptial vows are broken for reasons ranging from inconvenience to unwillingness to work through even the most innocuous of rough spots. Mutual friends, shared histories, and loving in-laws are cast aside with little hesitation. Divorces fueled by such differences are needless. A competent marriage counselor who respects the family could help put such differences in perspective. Yet some people haphazardly pursue dissolution without seriously considering the far less painful alternative of working things out.

The person who would prosper through a midlife crisis must strive to avoid divorce. There are several reasons why you should not try to deal with your midlife transition by divorcing.

## Reasons for Avoiding Divorce

***Don't divorce, because you will be harmed.*** Granted, many men speak of the euphoric sense of freedom that they have acquired by divorcing. Yet such claims are often merely a defense, with the true emotions being "despair and depression."[20] The distress following a divorce ranks close to the death of a loved one in severity. According to the well-known Holmes and Rahe Schedule of Recent Events, it is ranked second of the three most stressful life events.

You will be harmed by the painful feelings that may flair up for years after the divorce. For example, jealousy and loneliness are sometimes experienced when the ex-husband sees his wife with another man, enjoying what he perceives to be the fruit of his marriage. The man who has chosen to discontinue his marriage for less than noble reasons harms himself by sowing seeds that will cause him to feel guilty afterward.

After divorcing, your relationship with your children will be severely altered. Kids make a clean break impossible. You cannot fully put the past behind you and move on, since they will continue to exist and make some demands upon you. A weekend out of town or a vacation will be complicated by the fact that you alone must handle the problems, planning, and logistics that you and your spouse previously handled together.

If the children spend weekends with you, you will alone be responsible for feeding, clothing, and entertaining them. "Shared custody," that is, an arrangement in which spouses alternate weeks of keeping the children, is becoming increasingly popular. During the time you have the kids, you will have to do the work of both mother and father.

You may be hurt by your children's attitude toward your new companion. They may see the way you are treating her and think, "If he had only treated Mother this way, everything would have worked out." Tension usually exists between stepmothers and stepchildren which additionally burden the divorced father.

You will be harmed by the time wasted in a needless divorce. A lot of energy is spent divorcing, dating, finding a new mate, and getting married again, energy which could be spent more productively. One executive wrote, "My divorce was a pathetic waste, a waste of time and psychological waste. We could have stayed together; instead we chose to subject each other to all manners of psychological warfare."[21] Another said, "I just traded one perfectly good wife for another perfectly good wife. You sort of wonder what the point of all of it is."[22]

Breaking up your marriage may harm you more tangibly. It is now well documented that divorced men have a higher admission rate to all types of hospitals, including psychiatric hospitals, than their married counterparts and are more likely to suffer untimely death. One researcher, while stating that some marriages are obviously mismatches, also noted, "A surprising number of people fall apart after leaving what looked like disastrous marriages."[23] Usually included in the emotional toll in the aftermath of a divorce are feelings of failure and fear of another marriage.

You will be harmed by the fact that your personal problems will probably become widely known. Some feel diminished because, in the process of the break, their private troubles become public knowledge.

The loneliness you will experience after divorce will harm you. It has been theorized that the higher remarriage rate of men suggests they are more dependent on the marital union and suffer more from being single. The newly divorced man clearly realizes that he is not getting any younger. At a time when the midlife man should be enjoying the fruits of twenty years of growth and experience, he is no closer to settling down than a high school junior.

Divorce is harmful to you because you will likely have more problems in your second marriage than in your first. During the extramarital affair which often precedes a divorce, the flame of romantic love burns hot. Two adults find themselves feeling emotions they have not felt since they were in their teens. Their minds are preoccupied with one another, and they are oblivious to the rest of the world.

All fires must die down, however, and this one eventually does too. Then it is back to business as usual. At the end of a period of fervent romantic love, a little boredom usually arises and some self-questioning to the effect of, "Why did I get so carried away?"

When passions fade, problems surface in the new marriage just as they were present in the old one, except now they are more threatening. In fact, most who divorce can expect the second marriage to be more troubled and less durable than the first. Research indicates that half of first marriage divorces come within seven years, while half of second marriages come within 5.3 years.[24]

Second marriages lack durability because of the many difficulties which accompany them. Second marriages sometimes do not last because of the flawed characters of those involved. Remember, if you opt to leave your wife for someone new, you will be sharing your life with a person who feels little guilt over taking another woman's husband. If you leave a marriage that is not beyond repair, you will be bringing into the new marriage a lack of tenacity that may prove deadly to the new union as well.

Problems from the first marriage have a way of spilling over into the post-marital period. Difficulties arise over the relationship between ex-spouses. While many claim to "still be friends," few are. More relationships are characterized by acrimony than familiarity. Bitter disagreements develop over the treatment of children, times of visitation, and support payments.

The new wife may be jealous of her husband's attachment to his offspring. While he may feel he must spend more time with his son, for example, she may consider every hour with the boy to be one less hour with her. Her view may be that the child is spoiled and needs to learn that his father cannot always be there.

Financial responsibilities from the termination of a marriage with children can cripple the lifestyle of the new couple. Tension often develops when children from a previous marriage misbehave. The stepparent frequently has differences of opinion with his new spouse over the handling of such problems. Much time is consumed taking the kids to the appropriate parent's or grandparent's home. Children from previous marriages often complicate new alliances in many other ways as well. It is no surprise that nearly half of remarriages end in divorce in five years, and over 50% of those involve children from former marriages.[25]

Divorce will almost certainly harm your job performance, thereby affecting your livelihood. If you are self-employed, the pressure on your business from the distress you experience will be significant. A company's ability to remain profitable while the owner is divorcing is impaired.

As many sales managers will testify, the salesman going through a divorce almost always experiences a severe drop in commissions and sometimes completely destroys a client base through inattention. On jobs that are not sales oriented, productivity suffers. Even men who described their jobs as escapes from the emotional turmoil of divorce admit that their work efficiency declined.[26]

***Don't divorce, because people will be lowered.*** Individuals ordinarily characterized by integrity and kindness find themselves telling lies and losing their tempers. People of cultivation find themselves eagerly participating in "no holds barred" shouting matches.

***Don't divorce, because your spouse will be harmed even more than you.*** Wives rejected by their husbands for other, usually younger women, suffer intensely. Women respond to needs they cannot meet by feeling guilty. This being the case, divorced women are often tormented by guilt for years. They are at greater risk for acute illness than are married women, and they are treated for depression more frequently than their married counterparts.

Women react to divorce, not with a philosophical "he needed space" reasoning, but rather with a keen sense of abandonment. The anguish women suffer in divorce is seen in the suicide rate for divorcees, three and a half times higher than that of married women.[27] Far from being an experience of emotional growth, divorce for women is devastating.

Divorce may harm your spouse by impoverishing her. The evidence is everywhere. Look at the kinds of cars many divorced women drive and the kinds of neighborhoods in which they live. While 13% of the children in two-parent families live below the poverty line, the figure for female-headed households is 56%, the majority of which are left needy by divorce.[28] The hardship suffered by divorced women is so well documented that marriage dissolution is considered to be a major cause of poverty in the United States.

Sadly, in spite of years of legislation, most women can get only low-paying jobs with limited potential for advancement. The physician's wife who spent years "putting hubby through" may discover that she qualifies only for a clerical position at little over minimum wage. The college-educated woman who has shunned the work force to spend the last several years raising a family will probably find that her education is outdated and several refresher classes must be taken to qualify for anything beyond entry-level employment.

The financial hardship suffered by tens of thousands of divorcees is largely the result of liberalized "no fault" divorce legislation. Such laws fail to take into account the significant gap between men's and women's earnings. One observer, referring to those statutes, noted that the only ones to really benefit from women's liberation are men. Research shows that fully 70% of divorced women are constantly thinking about finances.[29]

Think about that. Now think about the woman you married twenty years ago. Clearly, any decision on your part to end the marriage is not a neutral choice. That therapist you sought out for help in making this important decision gratuitously tells you to follow your feelings. The problem with that advice is that there is much more at stake than how you feel. While you will be spending the rest of your life following your feelings, your ex-wife probably will be spending hers wanting for necessities. Has the "wife of your youth" done anything bad enough to be sentenced to an existence primarily characterized by a lack of money?

Your spouse will probably be harmed by being condemned to a single life. While men usually remarry in midlife, most women do not. This is partly because of the more frequent incidence of homosexuality among men, which reduces the number of potential spouses. It is partly because there are more women than men. The main reason, however, is that men tend to remarry younger women, thus lessening the chances of the midlife divorcee finding a new mate.

One survey concluded that a forty-year-old ex-wife stands a better chance of being killed by a terrorist than of remarrying for life. Imagine the deep sense of rejection women must feel when, after being rejected by their husbands, they find that no one is seriously interested in them. Many divorced people claim to be "friends" after the dissolution of a marriage. A woman might ask regarding her ex-husband, "With friends like that, who needs enemies?"

Psychologist Dianne Medved wrote, "When someone leaves a marriage without exhausting its potential, it should be called 'running away,' 'dodging responsibility' . . . Abandonment of a partner who loves you shouldn't be softened with words like 'fresh start.' "[30] There is likely no act of greater unkindness we men can do than to frivolously divorce our wives.

***Don't divorce, because your children will be devastated.*** They are harmed when reduced to poverty. Eighty percent of the divorced mothers in the United States receive no child support at all.[31]

Children of divorce are emotionally damaged by the lack consistent parenting typical of the aftermath of a dissolution. A father, moved by guilt over not seeing his children often enough may be too quick to reach for the checkbook when they are present. He may hesitate to exercise discipline during his limited time with them. The mother, in an effort to compete with her ex-husband for the children's affection, may likewise become lax with discipline. Children in college at the time of a divorce often drop out and thus do themselves harm that may last the rest of their lives.

Because they feel guilty about divorce, parents are often reluctant to exercise moral leadership. In fact, they may not even be there at teachable moments when such leadership can be most effectively exercised. For example, the best time to teach about the perils of drug abuse is when your son asks, “What are drugs?” The optimum time to teach the dangers of tobacco is when your daughter asks, “Why do some people smoke?” A father who only spends every other weekend with his children probably will not be present when such questions arise.

Fathers, unless they have sole custody, will typically spend far less time with their children after the divorce than they did before. Every father who is contemplating “starting a new life” ought to ask himself if that new life is worth decimating his time with his offspring.

Children know intuitively that divorce is not the way things were meant to be. Even when in adulthood, children feel very distressed when their parents divorce. My parents parted ways when I was twenty-one and a newlywed. With the responsibilities of having a wife and the demands of my senior year in college, the dissolution of their marriage was an unwelcome source of heartache.

We have heard of those who say they remain married for the sake of the children. That may be a legitimate reason.

***Don’t divorce, because the single life is not all it is made up to be.*** Some men picture themselves joyfully living morally unfettered lives. Things are not that simple. While newly divorced men may experience a variety of lovers, there are also long, discouraging dry spells in the dating scene which may last several years. Although being single again may seem appealing, it gets lonely and old. Forty percent of newly divorced men say that the singles life is wonderful. After two or more divorces, however, only 7% feel the same way.[32]

The man who divorces after twenty years of marriage may at first be impressed with the women he is now free to date. He soon begins to discover, however, that they lack the maturity and depth of his former wife. Additionally, in his zeal to court younger women, he will probably make a fool out of himself. Barbara Fried observed, "A man who at twenty is a young Lothario . . . and at thirty a dashing young man about town, at forty becomes, without having changed his personality or habits one iota, a roué who very soon will qualify for the ultimate distinction of being a dirty old man."[33]

One hindrance to the freewheeling spirit of the singles life is the spread of sexually-transmitted diseases. An evening's adventure can result in anything from an incurable case of herpes to contracting the deadly AIDS virus. One recently-separated fifty-year-old man said, "This is the worst time to be single . . . The mood has changed. It's not the outgoing, friendly mood it used to be. People are suspicious."[34]

***Don't divorce, because society will be harmed.*** Your split will say to others, "Divorce is not that bad." It may be interpreted by some of your friends as tacit permission for them to divorce and thereby contribute to the breakdown of the family upon which our society is based.

***Finally, don't divorce because you think "everyone is doing it."*** The truth is, everyone is not doing it. When one couple in a circle of friends divorces, it may seem that other couples follow like collapsing dominoes. Yet that is only the way things look. More than 58% of first marriages last over fifteen years.[35] In fact, divorces are much more common for teenagers and young married couples than for those in middle adulthood.[36] If you divorce in midlife, you will be the exception, not the rule.

Clearly, marriage dissolution is harmful and will cause many problems which will hurt others and drain the emotional, physical, and financial resources necessary to your prosperity during a midlife transition.

Terminating a marriage is not generally in the self-interest of the one ending it. Additionally, it bears bitter fruit in the lives of many others. What can a midlife man do to help his marriage endure? First, he must remind himself that the previously mentioned repercussions of a divorce are real and may ruin his life and the lives of those on the perimeter of the divorce. Second, he can show maturity by seeing beyond himself and taking steps to keep his marriage intact. He can remind himself that while no arrangement between two people is ever flawless, the first marriage is probably be as close as most will come to an ideal union.

## The Benefits of Marriage

Matrimony creates a haven from which to tackle the challenges of life. It provides something constant and dependable in an unpredictable world. While there may be strong disagreements, time has a way of diminishing the burning conflicts which are sometimes a part of the early years of marriage.

The man who sticks things out, smoothing the rough spots, will likely find married life very rewarding in the long run. Psychologist Dianne Medved summed up the case for staying together when she wrote, "Popular culture acknowledges that marriage makes you happier, marriage keeps you saner, marriage allows you more security, marriage makes you richer and more successful than staying single."[37]

It should not be forgotten that the institution of marriage was designed and ordained by God for the good of humanity. In Genesis 2:18 the Bible says, "And the Lord God said, 'It is not good that man should be alone; I will make him a helper comparable to him.'" The potential for love and closeness is so great in marriage, that the Bible compares the relationship of a husband and wife to that of Christ and his church. Ephesians 5: 25-28 states:

> Husbands, love your wives, just as Christ also loved the church and gave Himself for it, that He might sanctify and cleanse it with the washing of water by the word, that He might present it to Himself a glorious church, not having spot or wrinkle or any such thing, but that it should be holy and without blemish. So husbands ought to love their own wives as their own bodies; he who loves his wife loves himself.

The greatest potential for happiness and prosperity is found in honoring the heaven-ordained institution of marriage.

## Don't Walk off Your Job

Some are tempted to deal with their midlife crises by suddenly quitting their jobs. Before making such a change, a man ought to take a hard look at himself and make sure his employer is the problem. Wide mood swings are characteristic of the midlife transition, and neither the boss nor the job may be at fault. If there is boredom or despair over a position which has been outgrown, it is healthy to discuss the problem with your employer to see if responsibilities can be expanded to accommodate personal growth.

*Don't dwell on how things might have been.*

## Don't Dwell on How Things Might Have Been

Among the conflicting thoughts that enter the minds of midlife males are questions of what might have been: "What if I had graduated from college?" "What if I had finished graduate school?" "What if I had exercised more self-discipline?" Pining over what might have been is inappropriate for the man who would not only survive but prosper through the midlife crisis, for several reasons.

Such thinking leads to fantasies. One who finds himself thinking "what if?" may begin to picture himself in that hypothetical role. Daydreaming is unproductive since it provides the fantasizer partial gratification without any progress toward a goal. Additionally, it consumes valuable time. The person who would truly be successful needs to work on making dreams realities.

The "what might have been" type may think, "If I had achieved my goal of becoming rich, powerful, etc., then I would show my critics. They would really respect me now." That is simply not true. Just as some now criticize us while we are modestly successful, we will have critics if we achieve our wildest dreams. Some will claim we made it by luck while others insist that we were willing to stoop to anything for success. Some will sincerely believe they are better qualified and resent our being in "their" position. No matter how dazzling our achievements, some will refuse to be impressed, and will not acknowledge that our accomplishments stem from hard work and talent.

It may be tempting to think, "If I become company president, then I can pay those back who have treated me wrong." Yet that is not the way the real world works. First, becoming successful is not the same as becoming Dictator and Chief Potentate for Life in a banana republic. We cannot have our adversaries tried and executed. Second, no matter how far we advance, there is always someone to whom we must answer. It may be the CEO or the board of directors. The fabulously effective entrepreneur has to answer to his clientele. The famous musician deals with a record company which can refuse to renew his contract. Successful politicians must answer to their constituency.

If anything, the more visible our success, the greater the number of unqualified people who will be convinced they could do exactly what we are doing, only much better. Consider the vast number of potbellied "armchair quarterbacks" that fill recliners each fall and winter weekend. The president of the United States is arguably the best politician in the country, but that has not diminished the number of those who are convinced they could do what he is doing, only much more effectively. Clearly, accomplishment in any field—education, writing, business, art—will not make us omnipotent. If we ever achieve our fondest dreams, we will still hear the same types of criticism we hear now, only on a larger scale.

A person may be tempted to think, "If I can only become incredibly rich or famous, then I can indulge my every desire." That, too, is fantastic. Achievement brings greater responsibility which in turn takes time to discharge. Many successful people cannot afford the time for an utterly decadent lifestyle. It is usually easier to claw one's way to the top of the mountain than to remain on it, and much of their energy is spent in maintaining their position.

## Don't Get Lost in Activity for Its Own Sake

Many men in midlife crisis lose themselves in workaholism. Some put the career accelerator to the floor in a last-ditch effort to force the success not as yet realized. Others try to escape the melancholy that accompanies their midlife transition by burying themselves in their careers. Still others may have a practical reason—in a final burst of effort they endeavor to prepare for retirement which now seems closer than ever.

The last is the only justification for a spurt of intense activity at midlife for the one who wishes to prosper from his crisis. The early forties is the time to start working smart instead of attacking problems with a mountain of unreasoned effort. Much work done for its own sake unproductive. Time is limited. Care must be taken to efficiently plan how to improve life and then implement the plan.

---

[1]Gail Sheehy, *Pathfinders* (Toronto: Bantam Books, 1981), 145.

[2]Mayer, *Mid-life Crisis,* 185.

[3]Lois Tamir, "Modern Myths About Men at Midlife: An Assessment," in *Midlife Myths. Issues, Findings,* 173.

[4]Mayer, *Mid-life Crisis,* 29.

[5]Fried, *Middle-Age Crisis,* 108.

[6]Les Carter, *The Prodigal Spouse* (Nashville: Thomas Nelson Publishers, 1990), 17.

[7]Mayer, *Mid-life Crisis,* 226, 229-232.

[8]Carter, *The Prodigal Spouse,* 37.

[9]Herbert S. Stream, *The Extramarital Affair* (New York: The Free Press, 1980), 18.

[10]Ibid., 203-205.

[11]Stream, *Affair,* 87.

[12]Ibid., 171.

[13]Carter, *The Prodigal Spouse,* 131.

[14]Ibid., 43.

[15]Ibid., 70.

[16]Robert J. Havinghurst, *Developmental Tasks and Education* (New York: David McKay Co., 1972), 96.

[17]Walter Wangerin, Jr., "How to Say No to Adultery," *U. S. Catholic*, March 1988, 28.

[18]Constance R. Ahrons and Roy H. Rogers, *Divorced Families: A Multidisciplinary Developmental View* (New York: W.W. Norton & Co., 1987), 194.

[19]Medved, *The Case,* 20.

[20]Catherine Kohler Riessman, *Divorce Talk: Women and Men Make Sense of Personal Relationships* (New Brunswick: Rutgers University Press, 1990), 9.

[21]Anne-Marie Ambert, *Ex-Spouses and New Spouses: A Study in Relationships* (Greenwich, Connecticut: JAI Press, Inc., 1989). 181.

[22]Ambert, *Ex-Spouses*, 81.

[23]Michael P. Nichols, *Turning Forty in the Eighties* (New York: W.W. Norton & Company, 1986), 102.

[24]Medved, *The Case*, 129.

[25]Francine Klagsburn, *Married People: Staying Together in the Age of Divorce* (New York: Bantam Books, 1985), 245.

[26]Riessman, *Divorce Talk*, 152.

[27]Ibid., 10.

[28]Ibid., 6.

[29]Medved, *The Case*, 33.

[30]Ibid., 90.

[31]Nichols, *Turning Forty,* 101.

[32]Medved, *The Case*, 58.

[33]Fried, *Middle-Age Crisis*, 76.

[34]David A. Chiriboga, "Divorce of Midlife," in *Midlife Loss: Coping Strategies,* ed. Richard A. Kalish (Newbury Park, California: Sage Publications, 1989), 182.

[35]Klagsburn, *Married People*, xii.

[36]Rollins, "Marital Quality," 186.

[37]Medved, *The Case,* 188.

## Chapter 3

# "DO'S" OF A MIDLIFE CRISIS

*It is good and fitting for one to eat and drink,*
*and to enjoy the good of all his labor*
*in which he toils under the sun.*
*—Ecclesiastes 5:18*

While some "don'ts" of a midlife crisis have been examined, simply avoiding certain behavior is not enough. Positive, concrete steps must be taken to insure prosperity and growth through this stage of life.

### Realize Moods Are Temporary

Moodiness characterizes the midlife transition. In spite of his best efforts to look at the bright side and consider his age "only a number," the midlife male may experience bouts of melancholy. Despondency can come from the realization that time has permanently closed some doors of opportunity.

Dwelling on past injustices may contribute to moodiness. When younger, the midlife male was not quite sure if the wrongs committed against him were partly his fault. Now that he is older and more confident, it is clear to him that at times he has been taken advantage of and used as a scapegoat. He may dwell on having been fired or having missed a promotion at some time in his career simply because he was on the wrong side politically.

He may also brood over the failure of key people to help him at critical junctures. For the first time in his life the midlife man may realize his parents were not that good to him. Perhaps they did not discipline him enough. Maybe they did not give him the help and encouragement he needed to finish college. His parents might have failed to help him develop budding talents in his youth. Maybe because of their own selfishness, they did not assist him financially with his education.

The midlife male may resent a former mentor whom he now realizes was not trying to help as much as use him. He may resent his wife because she may have been unwilling to move for a promotion or because in some other way she let him down at a critical juncture. He may begrudge his children's tendency to always take and never give in return.

Feelings of resentment are sometimes coupled with exaggerated concerns about death. The reality of an aging body comes home for the first time at midlife, and that realization can lead to an almost obsessive concern about death. One researcher wrote, "During the first part of the crisis we tend to look on the dark side of everything . . . , and also to dwell at length on the two things that depress us most: death and dying"[1]

Midlife men in crisis often brood over death. The good news is that such grieving diminishes with time. In fact, as the transition approaches its end, when a man has even less time ahead of him, thoughts of death and dying are no longer as distressing. Additionally, he has had time to get feelings about relatives, injustices, and missed opportunities in perspective. By the end of the crisis, hopefully he will have laid the groundwork for a happier second half of life.

The pain of the first part of the crisis, then, is temporary. One must be careful not to overreact to it. Even though he may feel like walking away from everything or telling the boss exactly what he thinks of his job, such impulses must be resisted. It takes discipline to keep transitory emotions out of the driver's seat.

Such feelings should be allowed to do what for which they were intended: signal us that something is out of kilter and that the time has arrived for some serious changes. When they fulfill that function and nothing more, those emotions perform a valuable task. One researcher wrote, "The pain of crisis is the window to renewal. Renewal is a resurrection of unused potential. It means taking up again the program of self-discovery that we put aside so many years ago."[2]

The man in transition who restrains himself from acting on passing moods and instead allows them to be the driving force for improvement goes a long way toward insuring his prosperity when the crisis is over.

## Maintain Outside Interests

Men in midlife transition are sometimes tempted to conclude that a flurry of work is the only hope for advancement or improvement. They believes that some kind of quantum leap forward is the only way they can give their lives meaning, and they try to accomplish that by long, arduous hours of labor. They struggle to do in the next three or four years what was not accomplished over the previous two decades. In the storm of work activity family, friends, and favorite causes are left to suffer.

If twenty years of striving for a goal has not brought success, an extra ten to twenty hours a week for three or four years probably will not either. Actually, workaholism is not always fruitful. Some studies show that the workaholic is one of the least productive people in the office.

The key to a successful midlife transition is not simply working hard but working smart. Well-thought-out action aimed at specific, attainable goals and not a flurry of knee-jerk activity is what will produce prosperity. This will be discussed in more detail in the chapter on goal-setting.

For happiness *and* prosperity after the crisis is over, outside interests should be maintained during the transition years. Spend time with your children. After all, how much happiness can one have at forty-five or fifty knowing that his progeny are strangers who show little interest in seeing him? Yet that is what the man can expect who is not involved with his children while they are at home. Maintain old friendships and develop new ones.

Do not be afraid of the time church activities, a hobby, or club membership may take. Gail Sheehy observed that people who experienced the highest degree of satisfaction in life had a purpose beyond themselves.[3] Leo Buscaglia observed, "Genius often comes from being focused on one thing, but then again, geniuses are usually unhappy people."[4] Old friendships should be maintained and new friendships developed. More could be accomplished faster with a single-minded pursuit of an objective to the neglect of everything else, but the man striving to make his future rich and abundant will maintain a sense of balance.

## Learn Happiness

A worthy goal of a midlife transition is to learn to be happy. If we can find some measure of joy even though we have not yet become company president, or do not yet have a college degree, or are not yet earning a substantial income, we will *really* be ebullient at the end of the crisis when we have realized a respectable objective. How can we attain happiness?

We must decide to be happy during the process of achievement rather than at the final point of the achievement. Consider, for example, a college education. A person says to himself, "I am really going to be happy when I graduate from college." He struggles through years of homework, tests, term papers, and lectures longing for the time when he will finally graduate and be happy. After investing thousands of hours and a small fortune toward that end, the day comes at last when he walks up on the stage and receives his sheepskin.

He is happy—for awhile. After a few days or weeks, however, the warm feeling of accomplishment begins to diminish and pretty soon he feels little elation over his achievement. He sets off in pursuit of another goal and again imagines, "When I achieve this goal, I will then be happy." But we already know the outcome. He will experience a brief period of satisfaction when he realizes that goal, only to begin pursuing yet another "source of happiness" shortly thereafter.

The problem with this all-too-common way of thinking is that we spend perhaps 98% of the time striving for goals and 2% of the time realizing them. Therefore, the person who decides to be happy only upon attaining a goal will be unhappy 98% of the time.

We must learn to be happy with the process of achieving. Consider again our example. Acquiring a college degree affords many thrilling and rewarding experiences. It is satisfying to feel one's horizons expand and to gain massive amounts of knowledge in a relatively short time.

College provides a once-in-a-lifetime opportunity to constantly hear experts lecture at a nominal cost. Students in the course of their education can repeatedly visit a well-stocked library and explore their academic interests. They have the opportunity to discover their weak and strong points and objectively see their performance in comparison with others.

Collegians who learn to be happy with the process will have four years of excitement and character growth climaxed by the realization of their goal: graduation. Then they are ready to go on to the next challenge and find happiness in that pursuit. There is much to enjoy in the process of getting a degree or in realizing any worthwhile objective, for that matter.

Happiness results from adjusting to life. In order to grow and prosper from a midlife crisis we need to be ambitious. At the same time, we need to accept what life has given us thus far. If we utterly fail in efforts at self-improvement during midlife, most of us will still have relative abundance. One author observed, "Leveling off is hardly the worst thing that could happen to people whose standard of living remains the world's wonder."[5]

Those who find they are burning the proverbial candle at both ends should take steps to alleviate the emotional neediness accompanying their lifestyle. First, they should become attuned to the personal side of life. They can start spending more time with their wives and children and learn to enjoy slower-paced hobbies like gardening and hiking. Second, they should put time limits on their work schedules and stick to them. One may decide that, no matter what, he is only going to work forty hours a week. There may be a sacrifice of earnings in that decision, but time will be left for other things.

Happiness is found in doing what we enjoy. When younger, we may have allowed embarrassment to keep us from doing what we really wanted. By age forty it is time to lay aside such reservations. The late Malcolm Forbes wrote:

> The thing to do is to try when you get the chance . . . Instead of thinking it would be fun to try horseback riding, get on a horse . . . If you're down at the shore where there are surfboards for rent, try one . . . I don't care if you're sixty or thirty and you're afraid of looking foolish in front of your kids.[6]

Happiness can be enhanced by having an enjoyable job. The man in the midst of a midlife transition, after objectively evaluating his situation, may decide that another line of work would be more rewarding. If you can make a living at something that itself is a pleasure, by all means do so. If you do not achieve great financial success, at least you are doing what you like. Monetary success, if it does come, will be an even greater reward.

Finally, happiness can be attained by taking time to enjoy the free offerings of life. Emerson said, "If the stars came out only once every century we would make elaborate preparations for the sublime spectacle, but since they appear every night we take them for granted." As trite as it sounds, the best things in life *are* free. Incredible wealth and far-reaching fame do not make the difference between a life of delight and one of despair.

The most worthwhile and beautiful features of life are without cost. For example, there is nothing like a glass of cold water on a hot day. All can enjoy water, rich or poor. The wealthiest among us has appreciated the thirst-quenching qualities of water. Yet that refreshing and desirable liquid is absolutely free. The striking hues of wildflowers, a view of the craggy side of a high mountain, and the rich verdancy of a deep forest can all be enjoyed without expense.

I deeply love the seashore. The crashing waves are almost hypnotic. At this writing I am relaxing as I remember their sound. A trip to the beach is available to practically everyone. Granted, some stay in luxury hotels while there. Others own large, spacious homes near the shore. Some must stay in economy motels. Still others camp in tents and trailers. It would be pleasant to stay in a hotel with bellmen and room service responding to every whim. Yet the sea itself, available to nearly everyone, provides most of the pleasure. The wealthy oil magnate in a hotel suite as well as the couple of modest means walking along the beach can richly enjoy the sea.

Families are another source of joy, regardless of our level of attainments. A dock worker values his grandchildren as much as a stockbroker does his. A plumber can have as much fun at the park with his five-year-old son as can a physician with his.

While pondering things that are enjoyable, I realized that one of my greatest pleasures is waking up before anyone else in the family and reading the morning paper while drinking coffee. There is nothing exclusive about coffee and a newspaper; it is within the reach of everyone.

The simple things of life can bring much enjoyment. A retired friend enjoys going down to the local fast-food restaurant each Saturday morning and talking with his cronies over a light breakfast, an activity that nearly everyone can afford.

It is sad when a person spends so much time striving for material success that he fails to even try to enjoy the things that are free; when he works so much he has no time left for children or grandchildren. How pathetic is the individual who is so busy striving to "make it" that he can find no time for special moments with his wife. For real happiness, the adage is true: it really is necessary to stop and smell the roses.

## Take Care of Your Health

Midlife reminds us of our mortality. That we have used up more than half of our years is a strong and constant reminder that life has an end. We were hardy and resilient in our youth. We could go for days with three or four hours of sleep a night while struggling to finish a semester of college. A Saturday afternoon baseball game with friends left us a little sore but not disabled. Our stomachs did not respond to decades of unceasing power of gravity by hanging over our belts.

At forty we are vividly and visibly reminded of our age. Those reminders should not cause us despair but rather signal us that our bodies are no longer on auto pilot. Physically, we have entered a period of gradual degeneration. If we want to enjoy the good health and energy of a decade ago, we must take action. Forty is not old age; it is an opportunity, as one writer suggested, to reorganize our lives. It has been defined as the time to "stop taking your body for granted and start taking care of it instead."[7]

One of the best things a person can do for himself when in a midlife crisis is to improve his self-image, and a way to do that is to get in shape. Losing ten or fifteen pounds, building physical endurance, and developing discipline at the dinner table are excellent means of achieving that goal. Youth cannot be recaptured, nor can time be rolled back, but physical exercise can do the next best thing. Some evidence even suggests that working out can slow aging at the cellular level by increasing oxygenation of all cells.[8]

The first step to greater fitness is to take periodic physical examinations. Many doctors feel that an annual checkup is necessary; it is certainly a prerequisite to any serious exercise program. To be truly fit, plenty of sleep is necessary. A lack of sleep leaves us less able to clear the hurdles necessary for a prosperous post-midlife experience. It can also cause mental and physical breakdown.

We must control our weight. When I was a starving college student, I looked forward to the day I could afford to eat whatever I wanted. When that day arrived, my metabolism had changed and I could not eat many things for other than financial reasons. Who said life was fair! Sad but true, our metabolism slows as we age. Calories are not burned at the rate they once were, and much more of what we eat goes to our waist. We must be careful about what we consume. A high level of cholesterol in the bloodstream is dangerous. By avoiding certain fatty foods and dairy products cholesterol levels can be kept in check.

If we have not done so already, it is not too late to stop smoking. The dangers of tobacco are so well documented and widely publicized that one man commented he would either "have to quit smoking or quit reading." Each year 125,000 Americans die from smoking-related coronary problems and 100,000 die from smoking-related lung cancer.[9] Evidence of the danger of secondary smoke is mounting. Any tobacco user who is even halfway serious about having a prosperous post-midlife era will make quitting smoking his highest priority.

Related to the dangers of smoking and the importance of exercise is the need to take care of our hearts. Heart disease kills 550,000 people each year. In fact, heart disease and strokes account for 47% of all deaths in America.[10] Not only is heart disease a killer; it cripples. I am acquainted with a man who recently celebrated his fortieth birthday. He had a massive heart attack six years ago, and can now only handle light duty on the job—no lifting, no stress, no real responsibility. Obviously, his potential to excel in midlife is severely limited.

The goal is to emerge from a midlife transition more prosperous than ever before. The purpose of this book is to make midlife not the end of real living, but the beginning. That will be very difficult for the person whose activities to become severely restricted because inadequate attention to his cardio-vascular system led to heart disease. Regular,

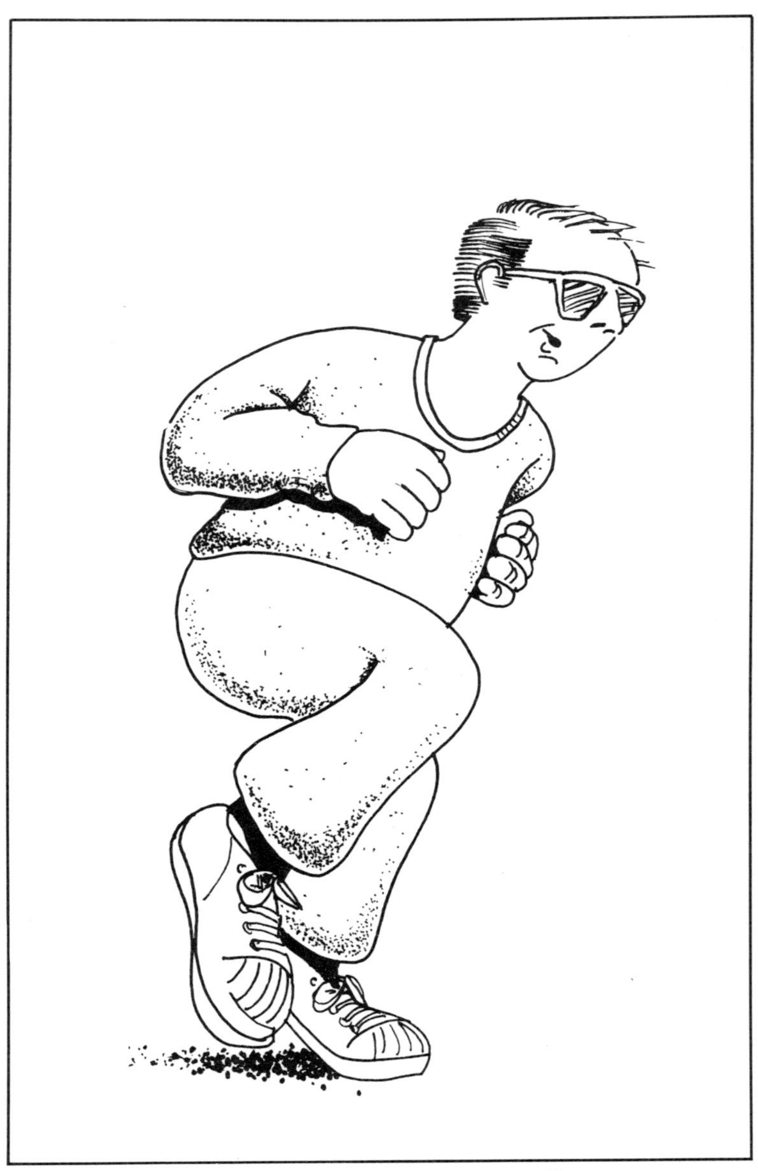

*Daily exercise will deter heart disease.*

aerobic exercise will help. A program of brisk walking, jogging, or swimming for twenty minutes a day, five days a week, will raise your pulse rate enough to give you a good workout and deter heart disease.

---

[1]Fried, *Middle-Age Crisis*, 66.

[2]Nichols, *Turning Forty*, 117.

[3]Sheehy, *Pathfinders*, 57.

[4]Dennis Wholey, *Are You Happy? Some Answers to the Most Important Questions in your Life* (Boston: Houghton Mifflin Co., 1986), 21.

[5]Shames, "Peak," 80.

[6]Wholey, *Happy*, 295.

[7]Fried, *Middle-Age Crisis*, 76.

[8]Richard Benyo and Rhonda Provost, *Feeling Fit in Your Forties* (Atheneum, New York: Collier, MacMillan, 1987), 86.

[9]Ibid., 165.

[10]Ibid., 38.

## Chapter 4

# GOAL-SETTING: AN ESSENTIAL TO MIDLIFE SUCCESS

*Commit your way to the Lord, Trust also in Him,*
*And He shall bring it to pass.*
*—Psalm 37:5*

Imagine that your slightly used automobile is a lemon. In spite of your care and maintenance, everything seems to go wrong with it. Then one day, while idling at a stop light, the engine suddenly catches on fire. While you escape to safety, the automobile is engulfed in flames. By the time the fire trucks arrive the vehicle is a total loss.

Hurrying to get out of the car and standing helplessly on the curb as it goes up in smoke would be upsetting to say the least. After your insurance company settles your claim, however, you would have a replacement much like the car you lost, except it probably would not be a lemon. What appeared to be bad luck at first would actually turn out to be a blessing. In the end you would be better off than if the car had never burned.

That illustrates the properly lived midlife transition. As you enter your forties you will at times feel distressed. It may even seem like your dreams are going up in smoke. Yet the intent of this book is to help you emerge better off than if a crisis had never occurred. Critical to achieving that objective is establishing goals which can be realized, or at least on which meaningful progress can be made, by the conclusion of the crisis period.

## Midlife Is an Ideal Time to Establish New Goals

As he tackles the task of setting and reaching goals, the midlife man has several things in his favor. He has matured to the point that he is no longer intimidated, or at least he should not be, by older men. The Cuban missile crisis was one of the most significant events of the Kennedy administration. A serious concern at the time was that the young Jack Kennedy would be bullied by the older Nikita Khruschev. Such was not the case, and the reason may have been that Kennedy was then past forty.

The Bible relates an example of a younger man being intimidated by someone older in 1 Kings 13. A young prophet traveled from Judah to Bethel to cry out against an altar erected by King Jeroboam. At the word of the prophet, the altar split apart. The king invited the messenger of God to come home with him, but he refused, explaining, "For so it was commanded me by the word of the Lord, saying,

'You shall not eat bread, nor drink water, nor return by the same way you came'" (v. 9).

As the man of God journeyed home, an older prophet met him on the road and invited him to his house. The young prophet replied with the same words he spoke to King Jeroboam. The older prophet responded, "I too am a prophet as you are, and an angel spoke to me by the word of the Lord, saying, 'Bring him back with you to your house, that he may eat bread and drink water.' But he lied to him" (v. 18). The ending is sad: the young prophet paid with his life for disobeying God.

Like that prophet, many young men allow themselves to be dominated by those who are older and supposedly more seasoned. Sometimes the tendency to acquiesce lingers into the late thirties and early forties. Perhaps your parents have had inordinate influence over you for too many years. Maybe your boss is overbearing. Perhaps a mentor who has outlived his usefulness still influences your decisions.

It is time to shake off compliant feelings and realize that half of life is over. Not that it is wrong to seek the advice of others. President Kennedy was surrounded by advisers during the missile crisis. It *is* time for decisions to be your own. It *is* time to cease bending to pressure from others concerning the direction of your life. It *is* time to become your own man.

As younger men, most of us wanted to please our parents. As midlife males, we realize that their job of child rearing was over long ago and we must now make our own choices. As younger men, we may have felt that wisdom is always with the aged. As midlife males, we realize that while there are wise old men, there are also silly old fools.

As younger men, we may have enjoyed the advantages of mentors who seemed to be genuinely concerned for us. As midlife males, we appreciate all the help we have received. At the same time, we realize that everyone has his own agenda, and some "help" may be offered because it primarily benefits the person giving it. As younger men, we may have believed that almost all advice given to us was good advice. We now know that some suggestions are good, and some not so good, and the best recommendations are usually the ones for which we have to pay.

By midlife, we have learned that when well-meaning parents sagely urge us not to move across the country because we will not be able to handle the weather there, they may be more concerned with how often they will see the grandchildren than with our lack of adaptability. By midlife, we have learned that the boss who advises that our greatest chance of promotion is under his leadership may be more concerned about keeping us in his department than for our career. The time has passed to live for the approval of others; we now must seek our interest and make necessary changes to enable the last half of life to be a rewarding, challenging experience.

Midlife men have reached a point of independence and assurance that allows them to confidently set goals. When I risked my life's savings to join the ranks of the self-employed, a friend advised caution, pointing out that "the grass always looks greener." It happened that the grass not only looked greener, it was greener. My income doubled in about ten months. The friend was simply reflecting a fear that kept *him* from taking risks. We must be open to sincere, useful suggestions, and weigh each bit of counsel carefully. In the final analysis, however, we are the best qualified to make important decisions about our future.

The midlife male ought to understand realistically his strengths and weaknesses. After twenty years of adulthood, he ought to know his potential better than anyone else. Midlife is an ideal time to evaluate new goals because it is characterized by greater objectivity. Most men were more dogmatic in younger years. In fact, some may have had an "all the answers" attitude. Now, however, a wider number of options for the future can be considered. Research supports the greater open-mindedness with which age rewards men. Advancing years have been documented as "bringing . . . increasing flexibility and openness."[1]

Midlife is a time to set new goals and give life a new direction because at this stage men are at their peak of influence in society. Power and money in this country are in the hands of the midlife male. He is a member of the generation that runs the economy of the nation. The man at midlife is at his most influential age. If there was ever a time at which he could elbow his way into a new profession, this is it.

He has greater discipline and self-control than at any time before. He is old enough to be taken seriously, yet not so old as to have his competence questioned. Couple that with physical strength that has declined only slightly, and the midlife man is in an ideal position to pursue aggressively a new place in society. Chronology, if nothing else, makes this the time for bold change.

The groundwork for an improved future must be laid at around forty years of age. By age fifty most men are too close to retirement to begin a new career. Additionally, at that age many are too embarrassed to have others know they are trying something entirely different. At the onset of midlife, one must begin sowing seeds that can be harvested soon enough to make a real impact on the remaining years of life. Levinson's studies indicate that the average age at which a midlife crisis concludes is 45.6, and, at the latest, 47. Changes must be initiated which will begin to bear fruit as the transition winds down.

With proper planning and goal setting most of us can succeed in that endeavor. Indeed, many have used the midlife transition as a lever to lift themselves to greater heights of job satisfaction, financial security, and personal happiness. For the transition to serve as a ladder to more abundant living, however, we need to approach goal-setting and goal-achieving properly.

Because of the substantial number of productive years left, opportunities for changes in midlife are bountiful. The person who is stalled on his job still has both time and youth enough to search successfully for other employment or seek a transfer to another department where advancement is more likely. If you have a talent for writing, starting at forty or forty-five will give you plenty of time to complete and publish a book. It will allow the market time to evaluate your talent. Midlife affords enough years to get an undergraduate or and advanced degree. It allows ample time to complete a Ph.D. and start a second career teaching at a small university.

Midlife leaves most parents time to get reacquainted with the children before they leave the nest. There is ample time remaining to reinvigorate a marriage or start a business. With talent, one may still develop commercially viable artistic ability, become an expert photographer, or ripen as an amateur actor. There is time to run for office, or get involved in a political party. There is time to develop a lucrative sales career, or purchase and establish a franchise. The list of opportunities is as long as the imagination.

The secret to success here, as in other endeavors, is to set realistic goals. The midlife man will want to use his increased maturity to accurately evaluate what he can and cannot do. We do not want to be like Jethro Clampett of *The Beverly Hillbillies* who planned to be either "a brain surgeon or a trolley car operator." At forty we have the experience to make better decisions than that.

## The Importance of Worthy Goals

Amazingly, most people do not have well-defined goals. It has been estimated that only five out of a hundred people can tell you precisely what they are working toward. They let things happen instead of making things happen. Thus by the very act of setting a goal, we place ourselves in the ninety-fifth percentile of well-planned lives.

Goals are vital to achieving any worthwhile objective. Roger Smith, former CEO of General Motors, said, "Once an objective is clear—and we should not proceed unless it is clear—we need to set reasonable goals to achieve that objective."

The quest of changing the course of our lives is a bold challenge; the endeavor must be met with dauntless, unwavering decisiveness. No one makes a "right" decision; he makes a decision and then makes it right. Many choices are self-fulfilling prophecies. If they are selected without resolve, we fail to support and advance them with the proper determination, thus predestining ourselves to failure. Once we have laid out a program for midlife success, we must see its accomplishment as imperative.

It is not easy to break away from the pack and do something different, yet well-considered boldness has its own reward. Just as an actor is not discouraged but invigorated by a little stage fright, we cannot allow fear to hamper our enthusiasm, but move us toward our destiny. One mental health professional wrote, "Sometimes I think there are two kinds of people. One group is weak, cowardly, and neurotic; they find change difficult and give up. The second group is weak, cowardly, and neurotic; they find change difficult, but do it anyway."[2]

Goals are the road map for the journey toward change. Without them, we cannot know how far we have progressed toward an objective. Goals tell us if we have succeeded or if we still must press on.

## Worthy Goals Are Selected with Care

The person who is serious about prospering from a midlife crisis will carefully select goals. Archimedes, the ancient Greek scientist who shouted "Eureka" once said, "Give me where to stand, and I will move the earth." Goals are where the achiever stands to change his world. It has been observed that "what the mind of man can conceive and believe, it can achieve." That a man decisively selects a goal and takes steps to achieve it probably indicates that he has the ability to make it a reality. He likely could not imagine it to be attainable if he did not have the ability to bring it about.

People who arrive at old age having accomplished very little have usually made the mistake of accepting mediocrity as the best they can do. One writer observed, "If they have always been a little bored or a little lonely, they think that is the way life is. That is all some people expect—and that is all they get." The midlife man who would prosper must rise above such thinking. He must expect more than a so-so existence. Setting goals is a way to excel.

It is natural to yearn for greater accomplishments. Studies show that midlife men in particular desire challenge at work. That finding gives the midlife male all the excuse he needs to set and meet new goals. Proper goals will not only be rewarding upon realization but will also provide stimulation while working toward their completion.

Because the goals we choose now will determine what we will be doing five or ten years, we must select them with care, then aggressively make them happen. Lester Korn, the executive search company head, wrote, "The successful are never passive. They do not just sit at their desks day after day and assume everything will work out for the best."

High achievers examine their lives and, seeing that they have a limited number of years left, firmly decide to use that time to achieve something significant. In doing so, they not only insure for themselves a more secure and satisfying future, they guarantee that the present will be dominated by the exhilarating quest of pursuing a worthy goal.

A psychiatrist wrote, "I have observed that a directed life is better, richer and healthier than an aimless one, and that it is better to go forward with the stream of time than backwards against it."[3] Goals keep us flowing in the right direction. They give us a target at which to take aim. Clearly, the person who would do more than endure a midlife crisis must establish clear objectives.

Goals have to be worthy to inspire success. The rest of this chapter will be dedicated to identifying the characteristics of worthy goals.

## Goals Must Be Realistic

My failure to set goals realistically at the onset of midlife was a mistake. In moving to Tennessee I had four aims. The first was to start and develop a business in Nashville while maintaining one in California. The second was to follow closely some stock market investments and try to maximize their yield. The third goal was to finish a book then near completion. The volume required exacting research and documentation, a time-consuming task. The fourth objective was to break into professional public speaking. To meet that goal, I would have to deliver speeches constantly for little or no pay at service clubs and chambers of commerce for at least two years.

Now that a few years have passed, rereading the previous paragraph is a little embarrassing. Leonardo da Vinci in his prime could not have accomplished all those tasks simultaneously. Yet I had never failed at anything that I really wanted to do. In the past, I had simply thrown substantial blocks of time at a goal, and sooner or later it was realized. Additionally, it seemed that with a shotgun approach, success would be realized in at least one of those areas.

As I settled in Tennessee, it became very clear that all those goals could not be met. I was in California two weeks each month, which left little time to work toward them. However, I did notice that during that two weeks on the west coast I was earning a respectable living. The thought then occurred that if I lived in California, two weeks could be devoted to earning a living and the rest of the time could be used in other pursuits. With that kind of time devoted to the aforementioned objectives, one or more of the goals could be achieved. I returned to California chastened but wiser. Upon arrival, I settled upon the objective of writing books. That was a realistic goal, and it has met with some commercial success.

A goal is realistic only when we are firmly convinced we can achieve it. Just as a salesman must believe in his product to sell it, we must believe in our objective. After all, we have to market it not only to ourselves but to others if it is to be realized. A midlife male who sets his sights on a promotion within the next three years must persuade his superiors that it is practical. That will require a high level of conviction on his part.

An insurance salesman who decides to develop a six figure income must not only sell himself on the suitability of that goal, but also his clientele, present and future. It is critical that we set goals with deep resolve. Words like "should," "ought," and "try" must be removed from our vocabulary, as they are often used for an "out" in case of failure. We must fully believe that our goal will be met.

Goals must be possible. We do not want to take the extreme position that we can do *anything*. A sixty-year-old man *cannot* win a gold medal in Olympic boxing. A fifty-year-old entry-level accounting clerk *cannot* become president of a large corporation. Educational opportunities may be limited, since some colleges have entrance requirements that do not allow midlife enrollment for some degree programs.

The cold reality is that the passing of time has closed some doors never to be opened to us again. Those who would prosper during a midlife transition must face this truth. One authority on the subject wrote:

> We all know such men who, against all odds, stubbornly refuse to relinquish a dream of becoming president of the company, or making a million dollars, or achieving fame. Approaching fifty, or sixty, their obsessive drive to make it big has locked them into a self-defeating compulsion to compete, or chained them to a suicidal frenzy of work activities."[4]

Realistic goals do not require talent, energy, or opportunity beyond what we possess.

While there are some goals that we cannot attain, vast numbers of opportunities are still open to us. Many middle-aged men have accomplished much. The midlife male should list possible goals and present them to a family member, perhaps his wife, for input. Often someone who knows us well can see whether or not a goal is really right for us.

## Goals Must Contain an Element of Risk

The reward of a goal is proportional to its risk. One might set a goal in midlife of, say, putting a swimming pool in his backyard or building a new house, objectives almost anyone can accomplish. Such goals have low risks and offer minimal rewards. Consequently, their achievement will not go a long way in giving challenge and depth to life. A goal that will pull us out of the doldrums upon achievement must be significant enough to involve risk.

Some have a dismal midlife because they are unwilling to take significant risks. The "play it safe" type often finds later that he has played it so safe life has passed him by. Midlife is a time to stick one's neck out, to put something on the line. The person who waits for all the lights to turn green before starting across town will never leave his home. A well-considered, calculated adventure can make life worth living.

While an appropriate midlife change involves taking a chance, it is not as great as the risk of doing nothing. By maintaining an unhappy status quo we chance "waking up" at fifty or sixty feeling that we have wasted our lives. Zig Ziglar wrote:

> When the ship leaves the harbor, there is certainly danger involved because, from time to time, ships do sink. But there's even more danger if the ship stays in the harbor . . . if it stays at anchor in the harbor, it will collect barnacles and become unseaworthy faster than if it is sailing the high seas, which is why the ship was built in the first place.[5]

Every worthwhile venture entails risk. Marriage involves the risk of having made the wrong decision and spending a lifetime with a person who was not the best choice. Having a family involves the risk that the children will "turn out wrong" in spite of our best efforts. The car buyer risks purchasing a lemon. Entering the hospital brings the risk of contracting an infectious disease. Renting a home to others involves the risk of property damage or nonpayment of rent.

A degree of risk is invigorating. It stirs and broadens. One author observed, "Inevitably, when we try to escape risk, when we limit our opportunities to grow, to soar, we feel more helpless, more dependent, more vulnerable—in other words, more childlike."[6]

## Goals Must Be Focused

Successful goals must be focused in order to be met. This is especially true for the person who is in the throes of a midlife crisis. A byproduct of the midlife transition is the tendency to make false starts out of impulsiveness. Obviously, the more false starts, the less time for achievement. They must be kept to a minimum by pursuing only well-thought-out plans.

Most goals for midlife achievement should be broken down into "subgoals," which then must be individually targeted. For example, consider a man who decides to get a Ph.D. in his early forties and teach at a small college by the time he is forty-eight. Our doctoral candidate will have to perform several tasks to arrive at that goal. He will have to find out if employment will be available once he has completed his education. He must determine which universities accept applicants his age and begin applying until accepted. He must begin and complete his course work, apply for teaching positions in various institutions, and move to the new area of employment. Once the "battle plan" is laid out, its separate phases must be pursued individually and relentlessly.

That might be compared to a man building a fence. First, he has to clear all obstructions, and second, dig the holes for the fence posts. He must then set the posts in the holes and build a frame for the fence. After all that is done, it is finally time to nail the boards onto the frame. Once the project is broken down into its components, he tackles the job one step at a time. Our fence-builder does not become anxious about nailing the boards to the frame when he is still digging holes. While he has the overall project in mind, at any one time he is sharply focused on one of the components which make up the project.

Earl Nightengale observed, "Just as a ship can only sail to one port at a time, set your first port of call." A pivotal reason for business failure is the inability to focus on one goal at a time. If we identify and tenaciously lock onto an objective, allowing nothing to sidetrack us, our chances of meeting that objective are multiplied.

## Goals Must Be Pursued Persistently

Our goal must be doggedly pursued until finally achieved. We cannot be satisfied with anything less than completing it on schedule. There are two kinds of people. One kind, as he gets closer to his destination and sees the light at the end of the tunnel, slows his progress. The other works even harder since he sees that his goal will be soon realized. We must be in the second category. A sense of relief in nearly achieving the goal should not be allowed to cause us to relax but rather spur us on with even more determination.

Even the most serious effort to reach a destination may become sidetracked. We may choose what appeared to be a main line but which proved to be only a spur. Veering off course should not be viewed as a disaster but as a signal to adjust our trajectory and thereby turn temporary failure into ultimate success. One author wrote, "The adversity and failure in our lives, if adapted to and viewed as normal corrective feedback to use to get back on target, serve to develop in us an immunity against anxiety, depression, and the adverse responses to stress"[7]

Temporary setbacks in pursuit of a worthy goal must not discourage us. Gail Sheehy, in her study of what she called "pathfinders," a cross section of highly successful individuals, found that over half had failed at a major endeavor. Yet all of them found their failure a useful, educational experience. She indicated that people of "low well-being" described a different set of responses to adversity, including overeating, increased drinking, pretending that the problem does not exist, and escapes into fantasy.[8]

If we are not now actively working toward our goal, we probably are doing things that lessen the likelihood of its achievement.

## Can Midlife Goals Be Achieved?

They certainly can be. It is amazing what we can do when we are dominated by resolve and determination. Many have accomplished great things at midlife. Machiavelli, while imprisoned, began writing *The Prince* at forty-three. Louis Pasteur returned to the lab to look at causes of decay in fresh food at forty-four. Richard Strauss composed all of his operas in his forties.[9] These and many other examples demonstrate that midlife can be the beginning of great accomplishments.

It has been observed that the bumble bee cannot fly; aerodynamically its body is too heavy and its wings are not large enough. The bumble bee, however, does not know it. If we can lay aside unjustified and groundless ideas about what we can and cannot achieve, we may discover astonishing potential.

Consider that over 80% of millionaires are self-made. There was no inheritance or rich uncle who gave them a coveted place in a flourishing business. They simply found a technique, method, or product that was profitable. Then they did it, sold it, or made it repeatedly until they earned a lot of money.

Whether our aim is to earn more money, become more educated, retire at a relatively young age, or change careers, others have accomplished the same thing before us.

One author, citing the rise to power of great rulers such as Cyrus of Persia, wrote, "They do not seem to have had from fortune anything other than opportunity."[10] Each of us has tremendous opportunity for achievement. We must simply mold and use circumstances to work for us.

---

[1]Gisela Labouvie-Vief and Julie Hakim-Larson, "Developmental shifts in adult thought," in *Midlife Myths. Issues, Findings*, 92.

[2]Nichols, *Turning Forty*, 116-117.

[3]Darrell Stifford, "Necessary Losses: Abandoning Some Dreams So We Can Grow," *Fresno Bee*, July 20, 1990, E-1.

[4]Mayer, *Mid-life Crisis*, 167.

[5]Zig Ziglar, *Top Performance* (Old Tappan, New Jersey: Fleming H. Revell Company, 1986), 234.

[6]Walter Anderson, *The Greatest Risk of All* (Boston: Houghton Mifflin Co., 1988), 26.

[7]Dennis Waitley, *The Winner's Edge* (New York: Berkley Books, 1980), 50.

[8]Sheehy, *Pathfinders,* 112.

[9]Jeremy Baker, "Tolstoy's Bicycle: The Best Is Yet to Come," *Utne Reader*, January-February 1990, 73

[10]Lester Korn, *The Successful Profile: A Leading Headhunter Tells You How to Get to the Top* (New York: Simon & Schuster, 1988), 55.

## Chapter 5

# MIDLIFE: TIME FOR A NEW OUTLOOK

*Old things have passed away; behold,*
*all things have become new.*
*—2 Corinthians 5:17*

A properly handled midlife transition involves a reassessment of our progress thus far. When we examine and find ourselves wanting, it is time to take a new approach to life. Liabilities that have contributed to disappointing advancement must be eliminated and assets that have produced attainments must be strengthened.

One author stated, "At forty, a man has reached full adulthood and the dreams of youth must confront the hard-edged reality of the present."[1] Based on that self-examination, the development of a new outlook on life with which we will live the rest of our days is essential. What are some elements of that new outlook?

## A Different View of the Educational Cycle

Western society's concept of a proper life cycle begins with a twenty-year block of education followed by a forty-year block of tedious work, which is then topped off by an empty time of retirement.[2] The would-be prosperous midlifer will recognize that pattern is not for everyone and that achievement comes from breaking out of it. The early forties can be a time for a fresh start with a learning period similar to the original educational period of life.

## Realism

For the male undergoing a midlife transition, it is time to confront reality. Feelings of disappointment which accompany the midlife transition force us to be realistic about who we are and where we are going. The person who has achieved only mediocrity is sometimes haunted by his meager accomplishments. While a bitter pill, that dose of truth can be good. Midlife is, after all, a time for accurately tallying the score thus far. It is impossible for one to take a new approach to life without becoming brutally realistic.

Deluding ourselves about what we will do in the future must cease because the future has arrived. Illusions about where the path we earlier chose will lead must be forsaken because by forty we have journeyed quite a distance down that path. We usually can see by now that it is not the best possible road to have traveled, and that it has limitations that we could not clearly see at the outset of our journey.

It is time for the midlife male to correct his attitude toward his tomorrows. Some live only in the future. They are so obsessed with achieving an important goal that they fail to enjoy the benefits of the present. Included in this class are those who strive for success or recognition to the neglect of their families. Ecclesiastes 4:8 describes such a person:

> There is one alone, without companion:
> He neither has son nor brother.
> Yet there is no end to all his labors,
> Nor is his eye ever satisfied with riches.
> But he never asks,
> For whom do I toil and deprive myself of good?
> This also is vanity and a grave misfortune.

The person who continues on such a course will wake up at fifty to find he never really knew his wife or children. He will find he never took his preschoolers out for ice cream, never had time to take relaxed vacations, and was always too busy to take his son to a ball game.

When in the throes of a midlife transition, I realized I had fallen into that category. I was so busy striving for the next rung up the ladder that my wife and family did not get the attention they deserved. Vicki and I were married over twenty years ago on a Saturday evening while I was in college. There was no time for even a day-long honeymoon; classes started Monday morning at 7:00. That hectic beginning set the pace for our life together. On one vacation to the magnificent Yellowstone National Park, I was at the pay phone in the lodge most mornings conducting business. During those years, I spent some time with my children, but not nearly enough. There was rarely the opportunity, it seemed, to help them with their homework or extra-curricular activities at school. The little time with them was spent grudgingly. I would have rather been working toward one of my goals.

The last straw was the short stay in Tennessee, when I was flying to California for two weeks each month for business purposes. When I got back to Tennessee I was so busy catching up there was no time to do anything with my family.

That area of my life demanded change at midlife. I have firmly decided I will not knowingly behave in a manner that will lead to future regrets. Now each work week seldom exceeds forty-five hours. A trip to the local ice cream parlor with my eight-year-old daughter is a frequent occurrence. The family has season tickets to the football team of my alma mater, and last year we spent about three weeks at the beach. I have invested a substantial amount of time helping the children with their schoolwork and take off from work to talk with their teachers and counselors when necessary. This is the most rewarding and enjoyable era of my life, and I am grateful to God for it.

On the opposite pole from the individual who lives in the future is the person who chooses the present over any deferred gratification. We cannot devour today like a starving man consumes a meal and expect to build a new tomorrow. If you long for a college degree, or desire to acquire an additional skill, your new approach to life must involve postponing some rewards to the future. The two or three years it takes to see the light at the end of the tunnel of a new life will pass quickly. You will be glad you restrained yourself in exchange for a better tomorrow.

## A Sense of Responsibility

A new approach involves accepting responsibility for our own lives. The individual who in his early forties is still blaming other people or circumstances for a disappointing existence will not be able to take control of his future. Winners make things happen and losers let things happen. Our lives are primarily the result of our decisions. Until we acknowledge that we alone made the choices which have brought us this far, we cannot accept the fact that we have the power to make choices that can change and improve our future.

## A New Disposition

A fresh approach may require a change in our disposition. Oliver Wendell Holmes wrote, "What lies behind us and what lies before us are tiny matters compared to what lies within us." We have all heard that some see a cup as being half empty while others see it as half full. In both cases it has the same amount of liquid, but the perception of the cup makes the difference. Some are grateful for a cup half full; others are disappointed over a cup half empty. The disparity springs solely from the attitude of the beholder.

What a person may perceive as personal failure might be a pessimistic assessment of his life. If an unduly negative outlook has contributed to feelings of disappointment at midlife, it is time for us to reinterpret circumstances in a way that will foster a more generous attitude toward our accomplishments.

Unrealistic views of achievement are foisted upon us from every direction. Television sitcoms rarely feature moderately successful people; typically they live in mansions. Fabulously talented movies stars, athletes, and business leaders are constantly paraded before us as role models. We may fall into the trap of assuming that if we are not like them we are failures.

One author wrote, "If a person's life is bound closely to society's notions about success, middle age may bring about disillusionment and disappointment."[3] We must be certain that dissatisfaction with our lives is based, not on unrealistic expectations, but on circumstances which can and should be improved.

## Sensitivity to Internal Demands

A new approach to life involves giving in to internal demands for improvement. As we have seen, a midlife crisis sometimes results from the feeling that one has outgrown his life. A researcher observed, "The painful questions that hit around forty signal arrival at a crossroads: A man has reached the point where his internal evolution demands a fresh burst of growth."[4]

Suitable challenges must be found to restore a sense of progress to life. Of midlifers seeking greater physical fitness, it has been said, "They pick for themselves challenges that truly make them happy, so that they are not overwhelmed by the hard work involved."[5] That guideline is suitable for those pursuing other goals at midlife.

## A New Demeanor

The person taking a new approach to life will begin to dress and behave like the success he longs to be. Books have already been written on appropriate clothing; that information needn't be repeated here. Suffice it to say that

*Midlife is time for a new demeanor.*

if attention has not been given to such areas yet, it is time to begin. Executive recruiter Lester Korn observed, "The sooner you appear to be successful, the sooner you will be."[6]

The person taking a new approach on life must carry himself with poise and speak with confidence. He must radiate an optimistic, self-assured demeanor. It is time to quit thinking of ourselves as over-aged kids and see ourselves as the grown-ups we have become—with the prerogatives and influence of adults.

## Responsiveness to Artistic Impulses

If creative urges begin to surface, they should be nurtured. If you want, take an oil painting or sculpting class at the local community college, or piano lessons. I recently talked to a forty-three-year-old plumbing supervisor at a large military base. He is about 6′ 4″ and must weigh 275 pounds. When asked about the song book on his desk, he said he was taking voice and guitar lessons. He saw that midlife is not too late to add an artistic dimension to life.

## Willingness to Take Risks

A new attitude toward life may involve becoming more of a risk-taker. People who feel they are in a hopeless rut are usually unwilling to take chances. Some are probably better off not taking risks; they may want to hold on to their gains. If you are happy where you are, you might be just as well off to stay put and enjoy the situation.

Still, many are not satisfied and their future success hinges upon the willingness to risk. One may expose himself to possible loss, but hopefully it is the loss of an unsatisfying way of life. To tailor a better existence, we must chance the possibility of failure. If a man decides to go into business for himself, he risks losing the money invested in the venture. If he decides to become an author, he risks the time involved in writing and marketing his creation.

The loftier the goal, the greater the risk. On the other hand, "Nothing ventured, nothing gained." A difference between those who live fervent, vigorous lives and those who find themselves in the same dreary circumstances year after year is that the former "overcome the hesitating attitude that is so characteristic of many of us."[7]

## The Pursuit of Job Advancement

The person taking a new attitude toward life may choose to pursue advancement on the job. Some when they were younger may have felt that if a person did good work, his job performance would speak for itself. Two decades have taught that Solomon was accurate in writing, "The race is not to the swift, nor the battle to the strong, neither bread to the wise, nor riches to men of understanding, nor favor to men of skill" (Ecclesiastes 9:11). It may be time not only to start doing our work well but also to begin making every effort not to keep it a secret. Lester Korn wrote, "If you are not already a star, how do you become one? 1. Do good work. 2. Make sure people know about it."[8]

The person taking a new approach to life finally may conclude his best opportunities are in maximizing opportunities afforded by his present set of circumstances. Change for its own sake is never helpful and should be avoided. Lester Korn wrote, "Most people, most of the time, *should* stay where they are."[9] He went on to say that salaries in most industries are higher for the person who stays with the same company for several years than for the person who frequently moves.[10] We may think we are stalled on our jobs when we really are not; we simply may have arrived at a temporary plateau.

Perhaps before seeking greener pastures, we should try watering the pasture we are in.

---

[1]Farrell and Rosenberg, *Men at Midlife*, 26.

[2]Mayer, *Mid-life Crisis*, 254.

[3]Van Hoose, *Midlife Myths*, 5.

[4]Mayer, *Mid-life Crisis,* 33.

[5]Michael Rozak, "The Mid-life Fitness Peak," *Psychology Today,* August 1989, 33.

[6]Korn, *Profile*, 131.

[7]Allan Cox, *The Achiever's Profile* (New York: AMACON, 1988), 160.

[8]Korn, *Profile*, 133-137.

[9]Ibid., 209.

[10]Ibid., 211-213

## Chapter 6

# RESULTS OF A WELL-MANAGED MIDLIFE CRISIS

*The end of a thing is better than its beginning.*
*—Ecclesiates 7:8*

The squalls of change sweep through the lives of forty-ish men everywhere. One who has allowed himself to be cast about by every urge and emotion will awaken at forty-five to discover that he has, at best, unproductively spun his wheels for five or six years and lost irreplaceable time. At worst, he will have made a shambles of his life. He may have two families and perhaps be estranged from one. In the recklessness that despair sometimes breeds, he may have destroyed a good career and greatly diminished his chances of again tasting prosperity.

The post-transition man may discover that an unnecessary divorce has left him financially committed on two fronts, with little or no money for vacations or other luxuries. He may learn that in the aftermath of a midlife crisis in which every impulse was followed he has permanently crippled his relationship with his children and erased the possibility of enjoying grandchildren in his old age. The post-transition male may find that instead of having progressed, he is back where he was at twenty-one. He must start all over, rebuilding the life he shattered in his early forties.

On the other hand, if he has used his midlife transition as an opportunity for growth, a man, as he reaches forty-five, will probably be satisfied with the life he has built. The latter outcome is the goal of this book. By sober, well-considered actions each of us can emerge from our midlife transition free from problems created by rash, short sighted action.

The tumultuous years can be used to lay the foundation for a more satisfying life after the crisis years have passed. Where will we then be if we use caution in handling our midlife transition? What can we expect after the turbulence of the transition has ceased and we find ourselves in our late forties and early fifties? Some results of a well-used midlife crisis will be considered.

## Good Health

The man who has used his transition well will probably enjoy good health. He will not have permitted the anxieties of the crisis to distract him from the important task of caring for his body. Likewise, he will have avoided the extreme of crippling himself with ridiculous amounts of compulsive exercise. He will have preserved his health because during his transition years he saw his body for what it is—the only vehicle to get him through life—and respected it accordingly.

Sheer determination can be more powerful than the body's aging process. Golfer Jack Nicklaus and baseball pitcher Tommy Johns were both successful well into their forties. Al Oerter, an olympic-caliber discus thrower for thirty years, finally retired at fifty-two. A fifty-year-old man can have the pulse of a professional basketball player simply by exercising regularly and moderately. He can enjoy greater endurance than a younger man who is not in shape. The groundwork for sound health in the late forties must be laid five to ten years before.

## Friendship

One who has handled his midlife transition well will have retained friends from earlier years. He will not have gone through an unnecessary divorce that forced them to take sides. Because he has preserved his family, the middlescent male will not be struggling to find common ground with a younger generation of acquaintances introduced to him by a new bride. Friendship accompanies a sense of well-being.[1] True friends of many years will be one of the results of a properly lived midlife transition.

## Growth

A well-lived midlife transition can be a time of profound growth. Rash decisions were not made that might otherwise have forced the midlife male to start over at forty-five or fifty. The post-transition man is not rebuilding a structure that was, to the detriment of all concerned, hastily razed only a few years earlier. If during his early forties he found that he had outgrown his job, the man in transition avoided impulsive behavior. Appropriate changes were instead cautiously and soberly made.

If beckoned by creative urges, the midlife man successful in his crisis resisted leaving his family to join a commune of starving artists. Instead, the gentle side of his personality was developed while real-world obligations were met. It may be tempting, under the overwhelming pressure of a straight-jacketed existence, to suddenly buy a Volkswagon camper and leave behind a mountain of previous commitments. The mature individual realizes, however, that such escapes are only temporary and end up creating far more problems than they solve. The responsible person has avoided flying out of orbit, knowing everyone within the range of his gravity would suffer.

The savvy post-crisis male refused to escape, but instead endured his crisis while developing alternatives that were not destructive to everyone in his path. Having deferred gratification, he now reaps the silent reward of growth. Midlife is a chance to "catch a second, and deeper wind."[2] So he could catch that second wind and use it effectively, the post-midlife crisis individual did not waste the previous five or ten years running in circles. Instead, he made maximum use of time and opportunity.

## Sensitivity

One who reaches middle adulthood having successfully negotiated a crisis period has emerged a more sensitive man. He now recognizes that there is a limit to what can be accomplished, even when the proverbial candle is burned at both ends. He understands that advancement is not the omnipotent goddess once imagined and that many of the best things in life really *are* free.

The unyielding self-talk that insisted "I must succeed" has been replaced by the realization that life is not one-dimensional. The man who has effectively dealt with his midlife crisis realizes there are other areas of success besides occupational and financial. Success as a father or grandfather, in his marriage, and in maintaining a good name are of great importance.

The sense of social responsibility in the man who has endured his midlife crisis is heightened. He desires to educate, train, and encourage those younger than himself. Involvement in politics is common to this stage of life. The middle-aged man has learned that diplomacy can be more powerful than brute force. He has become more introspective and more capable of seeing a problem from vantage points other than his own.

## Integrity

During younger years some find themselves in circumstances which seem to compel them to deny their knowledge of right and wrong. Much has been written about the corporate culture and its tendency to force even senior executives to endorse morally incorrect decisions. Some younger men are unduly awed by superiors. They may even join a chorus of pretenders in insisting that their "emperor" really is clothed.

The man who has weathered a midlife transition sits in the driver's seat of his life. He no longer needs a mentor. Peer pressure has lost much of its power. He now is truly "his own man." Having managed his crisis well, the middle-aged man feels little need to be someone else's satellite.

He knows that a career brings only limited satisfaction, and he is no longer willing to compromise his convictions for an advantage that may have at one time seemed as vital as breathing.

The man who has successfully negotiated his midlife crisis is not dominated by anxiety and doubts as are many of his counterparts who threw caution to the wind and acted on every impulse during their transition years. Rather, he has an active conscience and no longer has reasons not to listen to its dictates. He is too old to be bullied by older men with fewer scruples. The end of a midlife transition is often the beginning of new respect for one's inner voice.

Levinson wrote that men at this stage of life are "mainly concerned not with comfort and success, but with self-development and integrity."[3] In Erikson's eight stages of life, ego integrity is the last quality to be developed. The strengthening of that trait is fully underway in the middle-aged man. Erikson wrote, "The possessor of integrity is ready to defend the dignity of his own life-style against all physical and economic threats."[4]

## Power

While some physical vigor is lost by midlife, an offsetting gain of power is available to those who have properly matured. The midlifer's power over his parents grows since, as they age, he gradually assumes the role of "parenting" them. He becomes increasingly aware of the expanding distance between himself and younger generations; he does not have similar social interests and emotionally is on a different wavelength. Those a half or a whole generation younger than he is are keenly aware of the age difference.

That gives the midlife male the opportunity to exert leadership.

The man who has made his midlife crisis a constructive event is willing to accept the power that naturally flows to his age group by taking responsibility for himself and society during middle-age.[5] Researcher Bernice Neugarten wrote:

> Middle-aged men and women, while they by no means regard themselves as being in command of all they survey, nevertheless recognize that they constitute the powerful age group vis-á-vis other age groups; that they are the normbearers and the decisionmakers; and they live in a society which, while it may be oriented towards youth, is controlled by the middle-aged.[6]

## Ability

For the white-collar man, middle-age is a time when ability is at its peak. The decline in the capacity for learning massive amounts of information is more than offset by a general increase in proficiency. Verbal skill reaches its zenith in middle age. The skill to handle the challenges encountered in everyday living increases.[7] Experience gained from over twenty years of adulthood more than compensates for the minor decrease in mental keenness. That experience enables the middle-aged male to accomplish much more than a man in his twenties.

## Wisdom

As long as the middle-aged man focuses on what he has lost with the passing years—youth, strength, certain opportunities—he cannot appreciate what he has gained. His time-won ability to judge what is truly important more than outweighs qualities the years have diminished. One researcher suggested, "The optimum course for people who reach this first . . . stage of physical decline is to switch from physique-based values in their self-definition and in their behavior."[8]

The man who has succeeded in shifting the basis for his self-image from physical prowess to hard-won emotional and mental strength will find the post-transition era rewarding. One middle-aged minister, for example, found he could accomplish more from his office than younger colleagues could by driving all over town.

Cognitive functions, business dealings, earning a living, and getting along with the neighbors all become easier in middle-age. The person who maneuvers successfully through his midlife crisis is in a position not to dwell upon the disadvantages that accompany his age but to capitalize on the compensations which come with increased years.

## Confidence

The post-crisis male is part of the group that runs our nation. He is at his peak in many respects. He has the weightiest responsibilities in society. He is raising and educating the next generation, caring for his parents, shaping our culture, and producing the largest part of the Gross National Product. He is more articulate than at any time previously and, chances are, holds a position of greater prestige and influence than at any time before. Not only that, he has weathered the temptations of overreacting to midlife, thus having the confidence that comes with self-mastery.

## Conclusion

Each man who experiences a crisis will end up in one or two conditions. He will wake up at about forty-five and find that poor decisions have left his life in disarray, or he will emerge from the storm clouds of the midlife crisis stronger, wiser, more confident, and happier than ever before. A midlife transition can be a harbinger of disaster or a prelude to personal satisfaction and achievement. The choice is yours.

"Beloved, I pray that you may prosper in all things and be in health, just as your soul prospers" (3 John 2).

---

[1]Sheehy, *Pathfinders,* 208.

[2]Mark Gerzon, "Starting Over at Midlife: Why There's More Satisfaction to Life After Forty," *Utne Reader*, January-February 1990, 70.

[3]Levinson, *Seasons*, 243.

[4]Erikson, *Childhood and Society*, 232.

[5]Fried, *Middle-Age Crisis*, 116.

[6]Bernice L. Neugarten, "The Awareness of Middle Age," in *Middle Age and Aging, A Reader in Social Psychology*, ed. Bernice L. Neugarten (Chicago: The University of Chicago Press, 1968), 93.

[7]Sherry L. Willis, "Adult Intelligence," in *Midlife Myths. Issues, Findings*, 109.

[8]Robert C. Peck, "Psychological Developments in the Second Half of Life," in *Middle Age and Aging*, 89.

# Bibliography

Ahrons, Constance R. and Roy H. Rogers. *Divorced Families: A Multidisciplinary Developmental View.* New York: W.W. Norton & Co., 1987.

Ambert, Anne-Marie. *Ex-Spouses and New Spouses: A Survey in Relationships.* Greenwich, Connecticut: JAI Press, Inc., 1989.

Anderson, Walter. *The Greatest Risk of All.* Boston: Houghton Mifflin Co., 1988.

Baker, Jeremy. "Tolstoy's Bicycle: The Best Is Yet to Come." *Utne Reader*, January-February 1990, 73.

Benyo, Richard, and Rhonda Provost. *Feeling Fit in Your 40's.* Atheneum, New York: Collier, MacMillan, 1987.

Carter, Les. *The Prodigal Spouse.* Nashville: Thomas Nelson Publishers, 1990.

Chiriboga, David A. "Divorce at Midlife." In *Midlife Loss: Coping Strategies*, ed. Richard A. Kalish, 179-217. Newbury Park, California: Sage Publications, 1989.

Cox, Allan. *The Achiever's Profile.* New York: AMACON, 1988.

Erikson, Erik H., *Childhood and Society.* New York: W. W. Norton & Company, Inc., 1950.

Farrell, Michael P. and Stanley D. Rosenberg. *Men at Midlife.* Boston: Auburn House Publishing, 1981.

Fried, Barbara. *The Middle-Age Crisis.* New York: Harper and Row Publishers, 1976.

Gerzon, Mark. "Starting Over at Midlife: Why There's More Satisfaction to Life After 40." *Utne Reader,* January-February 1990.

Haan, Norma. "Personality at Midlife." In *Midlife Myths. Issues, Findings and Practice Implications,* ed. Ski Hunter and Martin Sundel, 145-156. Newbury Park, California: Sage Publications, 1989.

**Bank of Books**
2682 E. Main Street
Ventura, CA 93003
UNITED STATES

**To:** Main Address
800 Avondale Ave
1033647-1-1304
Grandview Heights, OH 43212
UNITED STATES

**Notes:**

**Thanks fo**

If you have any questions or concerns regarding

**Bank of Books**
2682 E. Main Street
Ventura, CA 93003
UNITED STATES
bankbook@pacbell.net

---

| | |
|---|---|
| **Marketplace:** | Amazon US |
| **Order Number:** | 1650997 |
| **Ship Method:** | Standard |
| **Customer Name:** | Main Addres |
| **Order Date:** | 7/8/2026 |
| **Marketplace Order #:** | 113-699090 |
| **Email:** | v1th1q1xndz |

---

**Items:**

| Qty | Item |
|---|---|
| 1 | How to Survive and Prosper: A Guidebook for<br>Langfield, Weldon<br>SKU: mon0000971449<br>ISBN: 0963409700 - Books |

Havinghurst, Robert J. *Developmental Tasks and Education.* New York: David McKay Company, Inc., 1972.

Hildebrand, H. Peter. "Psychological Problems of the Over Forties." In *After Forty—The Time for Achievement?* ed. Gary L. Cooper and Derek P. Torrington, 13-24. Chichester, England: John Wiley and Sons, 1981.

Jung, C.G. *Modern Man in Search of a Soul.* Translated by W. S. Dell and Cary F. Barnes. San Diego: Harcourt Brace Jonanovich, 1933.

Klagsburn, Francine. *Married People: Staying Together in the Age of Divorce.* New York: Bantam Books, 1986.

Korn, Lester. *The Successful Profile: A Leading Headhunter Tells You How to Get to the Top.* New York: Simon & Schuster, 1988.

Labouvie-Vief, Gisela and Julie Hakim-Larson, "Developmental Shifts in Adult Thought." In *Midlife Myths. Issues, Findings and Practice Implications,* ed. Ski Hunter and Martin Sundel, 69-96. Newbury Park, California: Sage Publications, 1989.

Levinson, Daniel J. *The Seasons of a Man's Life.* New York: Ballantine Books, 1978.

Mayer, Nancy. *The Male Mid-life Crisis: Fresh Start After Forty.* New York: Doubleday & Co., 1978.

Medved, Diane. *The Case Against Divorce.* New York: Ivy Books, 1989.

Neugarten, Bernice L. "The Awareness of Middle Age." In *Middle Age and Aging, a Reader in Social Psychology.* ed. Bernice L. Neugarten, 88-92. Chicago: The University of Chicago Press, 1968.

Nichols, Michael P. *Turning Forty in the Eighties.* New York: W.W. Norton & Co., 1986.

Nightengale, Earl. *Lead the Field.* Audiotape series. Chicago: Nightengale-Conant Corp., 1981.

Peck. Robert C. "Psychological Developments in the Second Half of Life." In *Middle Age and Aging, a Reader in Social Psychology,* ed. Bernice L. Neugarten, 88-92. Chicago: The University of Chicago Press, 1968.

Reissman, Catherine Kohler. *Divorce Talk: Women and Men Make Sense of Personal Relationships.* New Brunswick: Rutgers University Press, 1990.

Rollins, Boyd C. "Marital Quality at Midlife." In *Midlife Myths. Issues, Findings and Practice Implications,* ed. Ski Hunter and Martin

Sundel, 184-194. Newbury Park, California: Sage Publications, 1989.

Rozak, Michael. "The Mid-Life Fitness Peak." *Psychology Today,* August 1989.

Shames, Lawrence. "Has the Thiry- and Fortysomething Generation Passed Its Peak?" *Utne Reader,* January-February 1990.

Sheehy, Gail. *Passages: Predictable Crises of Adult Life.* New York: Bantam Books, 1976.

__________. *Pathfinders.* Toronto: Bantam Books, 1981.

Stifford, Darrell. "Necessary Losses: Abandoning Some Dreams So We Can Grow." *Fresno Bee*, July 20, 1990.

Stream, Herbert S. *The Extramarital Affair.* New York: The Free Press, 1980.

Tamir, Lois, "Modern Myths About Men at Midlife: An Assessment." In *Midlife Myths. Issues, Findings and Practice Implications,* ed. Ski Hunter and Martin Sundel, 157-159. Newbury Park, California: Sage Publications, 1989.

Van Hoose, William H. *Midlife Myths and Realities.* Atlanta: Humanics Limited, 1985.

Wangerin, Walter Jr., "How to Say No to Adultery." *U.S. Catholic*, March 1988.

Wholey, Dennis. *Are You Happy? Some Answers to the Most Important Questions in Your Life.* Boston: Houghton Mifflin Co., 1986.

Ziglar, Zig. *Top Performance.* Old Tappan, New Jersey: Fleming H. Revell Company, 1986.